After Caregiving Ends, A Guide to Beginning Again

Support, Suggestions and Stories to Help You Heal and Step Into Next

By Denise M. Brown

Thank you for buying my book!

© 2014 The Caregiving Years Training Academy and Denise M. Brown

All rights reserved. No part of this book may be reproduced or transmitted in any form or by any means, electronic or mechanical, including photocopying, recording, or by any information storage and retrieval system, without permission in writing from the publisher.

Published by The Caregiving Years Training Academy, Park Ridge, IL.

ISBN 978-1499150032

To my parents
(Roger and Sally Loeffler)

and my siblings
(Marianne, Dave, Keith, Barb, Tim, Jackie, Julie, Scott)

and my nieces and nephews
(Sarah, Claire, Kate, Megan, Patrick, Elizabeth, Jack and Matt)

And to Debbie Weiss and Karen Gurney,
who so generously provided their invaluable feedback

Mari —

We love you so much. You have cared for us & Mamaw & Papaw beyond measure. I know there will be hard times, but I wish you peace & healing & renewal. You have given us all so much. Take time to be happy for yourself and to slow down for your enjoyment. We're here for you. We love you.

Love,
Diantha Ann

Table of Contents

Introduction: 7

Close: 11
The Estate; The House; Debt; Regrets; Reconciling Resentments; Wrapping Up the Story; Working Out Worries

Open: 32
Outing Grief; Your Day; Your Routine; Your Health; Your Family and Friends; Socializing; Coping with Loss; Memories; Your Identity

Discover: 58
Your Values; Your Passions; Your Gifts; Your Purpose

Experiment: 66
Starting a Business; Writing a Book; Talking about Caregiving in Your Career; Changing Careers; Finding a Job; Volunteering; Relationships; Dating; Travel; Learning

Drive: 90
Stocking Up for the Road Trip; Managing the Potholes; Forming a Team for Your Front and Back Seats; Sometimes, Flying Past the Flaggers. Sometimes, Slowing Down; Handling Reviews; Changing Course

Share: 99
Your Lessons Learned During Caregiving; Your Life; Your Dreams

Read: 105
In Their Words: Life After Caregiving Ends

"I'm Okay" Worksheets: 155

Your Care Plan: 172

The Godspeed Caregiver: 177

Resources: 179

Introduction

I first began to think about life after caregiving in 1997 when I wrote a concept called "The Caregiving Years, Six Stages to a Meaningful Journey." The sixth stage—the Godspeed Caregiver—speaks to that life after caregiving ends. The end of caregiving leaves you a new person, yet without the time and perspective to adjust to that newness. It also brings up a conundrum—how do you move forward as this new person when you're missing the one who just died?

After Caregiving Ends, A Guide to Beginning Again accompanies you as you cope with two losses. The book will help as you cope with grief and that transition into a life after caregiving ends.

As a former family caregiver, you have access to information about grieving and settling an estate and selling a house. What you can't find is information about how to close out a caregiving experience. Caregiving ends in an instant and yet the the memory of the experience lingers. You may worry you didn't do enough to prevent a death. You may fret over discussions you didn't have with your caree. You might carry resentment toward family members who didn't step in to help. You might worry about the new make-up of your family; without your caree, will the family stay intact? And, you worry about finding another purpose as meaningful as caregiving.

Organized into seven sections, *After Caregiving Ends, A Guide to Beginning Again* features practical tips, helpful insights and comforting perspectives of former family caregivers adjusting to life after caregiving. The first section, Close, focuses on closing out the caree's estate and house as well as closing out the caregiving experience. In the next section, Open, you learn how to step into a new life, bringing along coping strategies to manage your grief. In Discover, you spend time understanding who you are now, recognizing that caregiving has changed your priorities and values. Experiment, the fourth section, encourages you to explore and try ways to apply your new-found priorities and values in a career, volunteering and relationships. After experimenting, you use information in the Drive section to choose a new life's path and manage those potholes you might hit along the way. In the section called Share, you understand how to talk about lessons learned during caregiving to help those family caregivers behind you. In Read, we share perspectives of former family caregivers about their life after caregiving.

I call you, in your life after caregiving, a Godspeed Caregiver. During caregiving, so much of your day was about you and your caree. In your life after your caregiving, it's you. That's really scary. It's also really empowering when you bring along the best lessons learned from both caregiving and your caree.

The book will encourage, motivate and inspire you to move into the next phase of your life, bringing with you the best of what you gained during your caregiving experience. At the end of the book, I hope you will feel comforted about your past, feel confident about your future and feel ready to begin your present.

(Note: I use the term "caree" to refer to the individual who received your care. And, the term "family caregiver" refers to an individual, like yourself, who provided care to a family member or friend. I have changed some names in the book to protect privacy.)

"There are always two parties to a death, the person who dies and the survivors who are bereaved, and in the apportionment of suffering, the survivor takes the brunt." ~ Arnold Toynbee.

When caregiving begins, you can feel like it's the worst experience that could happen to you. A parent or spouse or child receives a diagnosis—a life sentence. The diagnosis now makes your family member's mortality a reality because you have a name for it (the disease) and a time frame (the prognosis).

And, then the experience actually gets worse. You struggle to find the right doctor, the best care, anyone to help. You fight with health care professionals, family members and sometimes your caree. You don't sleep, you eat too much and you never leave the house. Or so it seems.

And, then in one moment, it's over. Not that you didn't know it would be over. You knew your caree was dying and would die. But not knowing when death would happen made it difficult to fully prepare. And, how could you prepare for the end when the experience still required so much of you?

But that moment comes. And, when it does, you wonder: Did I just lose the best of myself? In one moment, you lose a family member and a job. You lose the person who you loved and who became this precious focus of your day.

Maybe you had a love-hate relationship with the job of caregiving. You hated how much it took of you. But you loved how much purpose it gave to your day. And, now that it's gone, you can see how fulfilling that purpose was.

When caregiving ends, you have to fill two voids—the void left by the death of your caree and the void left by the end of caregiving. You're feeling the impact of two significant losses.

In this book, you'll learn coping strategies to manage those losses. You'll read how other former family caregivers move into their next stage of life, bringing along their grief and sadness as well as their hope and dreams. You'll also understand how you can leverage the skills you honed during caregiving to make the next phase of your life just as purposeful as caregiving. Throughout the book, I mention organizations, providers, articles and podcasts which may be helpful to you. You'll find more information about these organizations in the Resources section at the end of the book.

Read the book at your pace, moving into the next section of the book when you are ready. The book acts as your guide over a period of time. And, it's up to you to determine that period of time. You'll know what feels right for you.

About 14 years ago, Jeannette, who cared for her husband, Stanley, participated in my online support groups on CareGiving.com. When I think of life after caregiving, I think of Jeannette.

Before caregiving, she only drove within her town's limits, frightened to go beyond the borders of her comfort. After caregiving, she hit the highway, driving to meet those very friends she made in the online support group. She gave little thought to the distance she needed to cover in order to make those connections happen.

She faced so many fears during caregiving that she was fearless after caregiving.

You can, too. You can arrive wherever you want.

Let's go figure it out.

~ Close ~

"Grief is like the ocean; it comes on waves ebbing and flowing. Sometimes the water is calm and sometimes it is overflowing. All we can do is learn to swim." ~ Vicki Harrison

In one moment, it all changed. Death arrived and nothing will be the same.

Death, it would seem, is the end, which means that your sole focus can now turn to your tears and sadness. Unfortunately, the end continues after your caree's death. You learned this lesson during caregiving—it's all a business. Money must change hands, paperwork must be completed. And, so it is after a death. An estate must be settled, a home may need to be sold, possessions may need to find a new home.

Most important, an experience (your experience) must be reconciled.

As we look at closing out caregiving, you'll need something to hold on to, anchors that steady when so much feels unsettled. Embrace these anchors, which help keep you grounded:

1. Don't take it personally. It all feels so raw right now which is why it's hard not to take it personally. You take it personally when you think that what others do and say and ask is all about you. What others do, say and ask is about them. What you do, say and ask is about you. Believing that life is punishing you is taking it personally. Life may be difficult and trying and it wants you to succeed. You are being challenged but never punished.

2. Live life your way. During caregiving, you lived the best way you could so that you could manage your caregiving responsibilities. You sacrificed, adjusted, went without because that's what you had to do in order to make it. Now, you can step out from behind caregiving. It's all you. And, that's okay.

3. Give yourself the gift of time. Giving yourself time is not wasting time. You waste time when you give into fear, when you put off what you can do today, when you let doubts take control. You respect the gift of time when you take chances, when you give yourself time to heal, when you give yourself time to recover, when you give yourself time to make the right decision, when you give yourself time to find the right fit.

4. Strategize off the front line. A family caregiver, Martyn Feather, who cares for his mom shared this tip with me. It works in caregiving and it works in life after caregiving ends. When you're so mad at a family member you have steam coming out of your ears, you're on the front line. When you're so tired from grieving, when you can't think of a single part of your life that's going well, you're on the front line. Tears, fatigue, anger, frustration, resentment are all signs you're on the front line. Step back. Get a good night's sleep. Then, make a decision, form a plan, respond to a judgment. You'll regret a decision you make in the heat of the battle.

5. Some questions simply aren't for us to answer. You may question why you have this life, why you've had to go through so much, why you have to start over again. Trying to find answers to these questions will lead you down a long, windy road to nowhere. These questions may not have answers. That's okay. Simply accept your life; let go of the questions about it. You'll find peace in the acceptance.

With these anchors in hand, let's begin to close.

The Estate

Within 10 days of your caree's death, Consumer Reports recommends the following:

1. Bring the will to the appropriate county or city office to have it accepted for probate.

2. Assuming you are the estate's executor, open a bank account for your caree's estate.

3. Contact trust and estates attorney to begin the process of settling your caree's estate.

4. If your caree's home will be vacant, ask the local police to regularly drive by and check on the home. You'll also want to contact utility services to stop service and the post office to stop or forward mail.

5. Gather information from your caree's financial institution, financial adviser and life insurance agent.

6. Meet with your caree's accountant or tax preparer to understand tax implications as you settle the estate.

7. Stop payments from Social Security, other government agencies and pensions. When you contact these organizations to stop payments, ask about survivor benefits and any necessary paperwork and claim forms.

Your caree also may have digital assets (a blog, Facebook page, email accounts) which need to be closed. Contact each service provider to learn about their policy for closing out accounts. For instance, you can memorialize your caree's Facebook page so that family members and friends can share their memories and sympathies.

Ellen Rogin, CPA, CFP(r) and author of *Great with Money: 6 Steps to Lifetime Success & Prosperity*, spoke with me during a podcast about settling her mom's estate. "As a professional, I'm familiar with the process of settling an estate," she said. "And, I still found the process overwhelming."

She felt a huge sense of responsibility as her mom's executor and trustee. She woke up the in middle of the night worrying about taking care of the details.

When you meet with the funeral director to plan the details of your caree's service, you'll be able to order death certificates, which you will need to settle each transaction relating to your caree's accounts, insurance and titles. Ellen ordered 20 death certificates, which turned out to be more than enough. You also can ask the funeral director to help handle other matters, such as contacting Social Security.

Ellen and her brothers sat with the attorney together to get an overview of the process. If you are the executor, you can take a fee for settling the estate. If you do, make sure all heirs are aware of any fee you take and that you keep all receipts and document all expenses.

When you meet with professionals, such as attorneys and financial planners, Ellen suggests asking: "What do I have to do right away? What needs my immediate attention?" Often, details can be handled over a period of time, rather than immediately. Take an accounting of the value of your caree's assets twice--at the date of your caree's death and when assets get distributed.

Take time to make decisions, Ellen suggested. When you are overwhelmed, give yourself a night's sleep and a chance to talk it out with professionals before making a decision or taking action. "Get support and people to help you," Ellen said.

Settling her mom's estate took Ellen about six months. It's important to communicate with family members that the process will take time. And, share regular updates so heirs and other family members don't make assumptions about the process. Ellen remembered her brother complaining when the process reached three months. In Ellen's mind, she was grateful how much she had accomplished at three months. Ongoing communication will ensure everyone understands where you are in the process.

As you liquidate assets, you'll need to complete required forms from each institution. After you request the forms, expect to follow up in order to actually receive the forms you'll need to complete the transactions. Policies about liquidating assets differ from company to company so be sure to ask questions if a process seems confusing. Offload paperwork as you can, although be sure to check with financial institutions about the fees involved if you ask them to take over managing the paperwork.

Know:
a. It's overwhelming. Do what you can to reduce the upset—get help and support.
b. Consider hiring a bookkeeper for accounting purposes.
c. Ask questions (including the same questions) as often as you need.

"Figure out a way to take care of yourself during the process," Ellen recommended.

As you close out the estate, make financial decision based on facts not emotions. A trusted set of professionals helping you ensures you stay on track and that you're not intimated by the experience and any family members who put pressure on you.

After you have settled the estate, consider putting your own paperwork in order, if you haven't already. You now have a clear picture of the importance of an organized estate and detailed end-of-life wishes. Meet with an attorney to create your will, your durable Power of Attorney for health care and finance and, if appropriate, trusts. Be sure family members have copies of your important paperwork and that you've clearly expressed your wishes to them.

"I created all of these documents shortly after my mother's death," said Karen Gurney. "I put them in a labeled blue notebook which is in an easy-to-find spot and gave copes to the kids and discussed it with them.

"My mother did this after my father's death," Karen added. "Even though she lived many more healthy, productive years, this was such a blessing to me and to my siblings. How else would I have known that she wanted a green coffin?"

The House

You may have a home to sell after caregiving which means you also have a house to clean out.

During a podcast interview with me, Julie Hall, author of *The Boomer Burden: Dealing with Your Parents' Lifetime Accumulation of Stuff*, shared a process to help you get through the house. Start in the attic, then move to the closets with clothing, then to the kitchen cabinets. End your clean sweep in the garage and then the basement. Sort the stuff into four piles you've created: Discard, Donate, Sell and Keep.

Before discarding or giving away clothes, be sure to check pockets for any money. My great uncle stuffed apron pockets with money, which my father discovered when cleaning out his apartment. And, before throwing out any contents of the freezer, unwrap contents to ensure your caree hasn't hidden money. I've heard stories of what appeared to be frozen meat turning out to be stacks of money.

The house's clutter may feel overwhelming—until other family members arrive. There's something about a house full of possessions that brings out the vultures. I've heard horror stories of other family members clearing out a house of its possessions at night, leaving the family caregivers open-mouthed the next morning as they stand in an empty house. It's not easy to clear out a house when your family members appear with their own agendas.

Family members may suddenly battle you for your caree's favorite possession. You couldn't imagine they would show up now because they never showed up before. You might kick yourself that you didn't take what you wanted before. You may fear you'll never get what you want now.

When working with family members to clean out a house, Julie offered the following suggestions to help:

1. Check your expectations at the door.
2. Lead with kindness and compassion.
3. Make a pact: Let's not fight. Instead, choose compromises.
4. Be open-minded to what others want.
5. Hire an objective third-party to appraise the valuables.
6. Ask each heir to create a wish list, which can help with distribution.
7. Promote peace.

You may find yourself and another family member wrangling to get the family silver. To help with decisions about who gets what, Marlene S. Stum, Extension Specialist and Professor — Family Social Science, and author of *Who Gets Grandma's Yellow Pie Plate*, suggests the following:

1. Recognize that **decisions about personal belongings are often more challenging than decisions about titled property**. Assuming such decisions are unimportant or trivial can lead to misunderstandings and conflicts.
2. **Consider how to deal with conflicts before they arise**. Issues of power and control do not disappear in inheritance decisions. Unresolved conflicts among parents, adult

children, siblings, and others are often at the heart of what goes wrong with inheritance decisions. Listen for feelings and emotions, watch for blaming, and determine if you can agree to disagree if conflicts arise.
3. Remember that **different perceptions of what's "fair" are normal and should be expected**. Those involved need to uncover the unwritten rules and assumptions about fairness that exist among family members.
4. **Consider all options**. Being fair does not always mean being equal. In fact, dividing personal property equally is sometimes impossible.
5. **Ask others for input**. Individuals who have input and agree on how decisions are made are more likely to feel the outcomes of those decisions are fair.
6. **Discuss what those involved want to accomplish**. This will help reduce mistaken assumptions, misunderstood intentions, and makes choosing distribution options easier.
7. **Ask others to identify items that have special meaning to them**. This will help minimize inaccurate assumptions about who should get what. Not everyone will find the same items meaningful.

In his book, *The Four Agreements, A Practical Guide to Personal Freedom*, Don Miguel Ruiz shares his tenets on how to get along with others. He suggests you create these agreements in your interpersonal relationships:

1. Never assume.
2. Don't take things personally.
3. Be impeccable with your word.
4. Do your best.

Don Miguel Ruiz's book will really come in handy when you're dealing with your caree's inheritance, including the possessions. His suggestions on how to conduct yourself within your relationships will be a welcome guide as you move through greed, jealousy, selfishness and self-centeredness. Fighting over possessions and money will bring out the worst in others —decide you can be above that. If the fighting escalates and you feel the situation has become abusive, get help from an attorney or a therapist. They can help you set limits and boundaries and put a system in place to protect you.

Consider Pam, who watched her husband's family fracture over her mother-in-law's possessions. Pam's sister-in-law, Sandy, was the executor of the estate. She took her role to a new level, fighting with her two brothers over her mother's decisions about division of assets. The final break occurred when she kept a beloved family heirloom from Pam's daughter, who had been promised the heirloom by her grandmother. The estate did settle, but only after the attorney bills piled up and bad feelings festered. The family ultimately splintered, with the two brothers remaining on good terms while the sister retreated away in silence for years.

Pam did her best to keep in touch with Sandy's adult children as Sandy remained estranged and separate from the family. Years after her mother's death, Sandy reached out to the family after her husband's diagnosis of cancer and before her son married. The family reunited at the wedding and now keeps in touch with Sandy as she cares for her husband. Although the beloved heirloom is still not where it needs to be, the cold hearts have warmed.

During these upsetting disagreements, you may be prepared to permanently end a relationship because of a disagreement over a caree's possessions. Instead decide to take a break. Maybe the break lasts for 10 years but keeping that outlook ("this is temporary") means you'll be able to welcome back those who walked away when they return.

As you clear out the house and everyone gets their possessions, be open to the idea of the new fair that Marlene Stum suggests. Chances are, you'll watch as some receive when they never gave. This will drive you nuts—and understandably so. Understand that you don't have to judge what's fair, that it's okay if the distribution system seems unfair.

I often give a presentation about giving away your personal possessions while you're alive. During the presentation, I hear the stories of how possessions have been passed down in the family. And, typically, a story comes out about the unfairness of who got what. Anne, who attended one of these workshops, shared a story about her mom's good china, a prized possession that her mom left to her brother (her mom's only son) and his wife. The wife never used the china, choosing instead to store it in the rafters of her garage. This made Anne crazy.

During the presentation, we talked about ways to bring the china back into use within the family. For instance, Anne could ask to store the china so it could be used for family get-togethers. She also could ask her sister-in-law to bring certain pieces to family get-togethers. She also could ask her brother if the china could be passed between Anne, another sister and her brother, with Anne receiving the china during the holidays she hosts. Rather than asking her brother why his wife doesn't use the china, Anne can present solutions to put the china back in circulation. She may have more tweaking and compromising to do but if she focuses on using the china, rather than lashing out at her sister-in-law, she'll find a solution that works.

During this presentation about passing on possessions, attendees will worry about the next generation not wanting these possessions. If you find yourself looking at a house full of what no one wants, then move into the next options: Hire a company to hold an estate sale, manage your own garage sale, or simply donate possessions and furniture to charities. Do not take this personally and do not make it personal; don't inflict guilt on others or yourself. It's okay if you can't keep it all and it's okay if others don't want it. Your caree enjoyed the possessions during his or her lifetime; focus on that.

During the struggle over the possessions, remind yourself that you've already won the greatest inheritance you ever could. When the battle begins over your caree's baseball card collection or costume jewelry, enter the fight when it's really important for you. If you lose a possession you really wanted, know you can keep the possession in other ways. Look for photos, write out the story of the possession, journal about the meaning of the possession to you.

Otherwise, put your attention on the inheritance that's really important: Document your favorite memories of your caree. You'll want to capture your memories while they are fresh, which is now. Write the memories in a journal, in a Word document or record them in series of videos. When you think about what you get from your caree, know that the stories you've gained will be one of your greatest treasures. Make sure you take care of them by recording them now.

Perhaps you and your caree shared a home and now you must clear out the home and move.

When you pack up the house, be sure to have help around you. You may feel like it's a bother to ask others to help you pack up the house. It can be a very sad, tiring and difficult task to pack up your home (which feels like your life). It's important you have others who can offer comfort, keep the packing moving along and keep you company during breaks. You also can hire a service, like a senior move manager, to pack and move you. A packing and moving service can even unpack and organize your new place so you only have to show up at the end of the day to admire your new home. Whatever you need to make the packing and moving less difficult, do it.

Rather than selling a home, you may be staying in your home but wonder how so much of the house got lost to caregiving. After your caree's death, so much goes out of the door— medical equipment, supplies, even people, like the home health aides who took over so many of the rooms. You may have reconfigured the house because of caregiving, turning living rooms into bedrooms, closets into almost supply warehouses. How do you transform a hospital back into a home?

As with all transitions, give yourself time and permission. If you are ready to move furniture back into its original place the weekend after your caree's death, go for it. If you need to close doors for awhile, do that. If you need support to figure out how to put the house back together, do that. I connected with an individual on Twitter who shared that another sister helped their sister put the house back together five months after her husband's death. The sister who stepped in was pleasant and matter-of-fact about the task, which made the experience easier for the grieving sister.

You can turn the house back into how it looked before caregiving. Or, you can change everything around. Or, you change everything around and then turn it back to how it looked before caregiving. You can ask family members and friends for suggestions and ideas. Or, not.

My only caveat: If you live with others, be open to the impact of your decisions on them. Will it help your family move forward if you decide together how to transform the house? And, know that changing the home doesn't change the love you hold for your caree. You're changing the house, not your heart. Make the house work for you and your family at this point in time.

The experience of putting the house back together can be cathartic. Honor, treasure and then give yourself a new start.

Debt

If your caree dies with debt, your caree's estate is liable for the debt unless you have co-signed the loan, such as for a mortgage or credit card. After your caree's death, do not use his or her credit cards. Instead, cut them up and send them with a copy of the death certificate to the three credit reporting bureaus (TransUnion, Equifax and Experian). You also can check with the credit card companies about insurance for the cards which would cover the debt after a death.

If your caree dies with more debts than assets, the state probate court will determine which creditors will receive payments. Before paying any bills and settling any debts, consult with your financial adviser. And, again, as long the debt is only in your caree's name, you are not liable for paying back the debt.

Caregiving is expensive, which means you may have bills to pay or debt that you carry. If you struggle to pay your bills, contact your creditors and explain your situation. Ask to work out a payment plan. If you can't reach an agreement with your creditors, check into credit counseling. Before you pursue bankruptcy, consider all your options and talk about those options with a trusted adviser.

If you feel you can manage your debts, then work out a plan to pay them off. Some people like to focus on paying off one credit card at a time, making a larger payment toward one card and just paying the minimum on others. Dave Ramsey, of the nationally-syndicated radio show, The Dave Ramsey Show, and author of *The Total Money Makeover*, suggests paying off your smallest debts first, which helps you experience early success, building momentum to keep you going.

I believe the worst approach you can take toward your debt is to feel shame about it. There's no shame in trying to do your best and often times financial debt is part of that. Talk it out with others, look for ways to get support and then be honest about the debt. Maybe you know you owe on six credit cards but you're not sure of the exact amount. Sit down and figure out the total. When you know how much you owe, you can start to formalize your plan and consider your options.

And, be honest about your debt with family members and friends. Everyone understands a budget and everyone respects the individual who spends within a budget. When it's time to give gifts because of a holiday or birthday, simply say: "I have a really tight budget because of my debt. To celebrate your birthday, could I have you over for dinner?"

Keep plugging away at your debt; your small steps today will pay off for you in the future

Regrets

A visitor to my website, posted this comment in response to my question, "What Can a Family Caregiver Do To Prevent Regrets?":

"A few months after his death, which happened at home at 2:30 a.m., and after four years of his being bedridden and requiring a lift for all transfers, I still do know that a better person would have done it all better, anticipated his needs better, even created a better memorial for him. I just cannot get over, in retrospect, the alarming ways in which I failed such a kind and generous spirit. He has left me without cares, yet I know that I had failed him so miserably. In the end, however, I do believe that he knew that he was loved, even if he loved himself less for his disabilities. And I believe that he is happy now–not just happy but soaring. Perhaps he received extra points in heaven for my ineptitude. Godspeed and thank God that we are merely human beings for a reason."

When caregiving ends, you may find yourself full of time. And, with the time, comes the replay of events. You may wonder about a decision, or a comment, or an action. You may feel that you didn't do enough to keep your caree alive, that you didn't ask the right question, choose the right option, opt for the right treatment, see the signs.

In essence, it's your fault your caree died.

The reality of caregiving is that you more than likely saved your caree's life several times. Which can lead you to believe that you could always keep your caree going. We aren't meant to live forever, which is why we don't. And, a caree's death is not because of you—it's because of the natural cycle of life.

During a podcast interview, Janet Cromer, author of *Professor Cromer Learns to Read: A Couple's New Life after Brain Injury*, shared the story of a gridler, a kitchen gadget she purchased with the intent of using while Alan, her husband and her caree, was alive. Five months after Alan's death during a kitchen reorganization, she discovered the gridler in its original box. The gridler meant guilt—she had meant to make the blueberry pancakes Alan so loved and the fancy sandwiches that would brighten their days. During his last months, she had forgotten she had the gridler and didn't unpack it. She felt guilty that she hadn't done "the nice things" to make his day easier.

She brought up this gridler—the "vessel of guilt and regret"--during a bereavement support group. It represented the pain of their past and of her future. She didn't do enough during his life. She couldn't save him and keep him from suffering. And, she couldn't right the past in the future because he was gone.
Eventually, as Janet worked through the guilt by talking it out and writing in her journal, she unpacked the gridler to prepare a meal for a good friend. She felt she made a huge step forward when she could use the gridler without apologizing to Alan.

You may feel you must live with regrets that you've lost the chance to apologize to your caree for what you couldn't or didn't do. You may now believe you should have been more patient, more understanding, more available, more loving. Whatever you did, you may regret that you didn't do more.

You may also find yourself horrified at those thoughts you had about your caree during difficult moments. During a tough day, you may have had thoughts that verged on hatred. Now, you may think: How awful I was. What a horrible person I was.

A former family caregiver shared about a situation that happened as he cared for his wife. After a long hospitalization, his wife returned home with a ventilator. Her family disagreed with his decision to bring his wife home so he was on his own. The first night they were home, she woke him at 3:30 a.m. because she couldn't breathe. Overwhelmed and frantic, he reacted in a way he wish he hadn't. He finally fixed the problem by adjusting her breathing tube. But the regret at his initial reaction still lives with him.

Part of closing out regrets means forgiving yourself for simply being human. Of course you often didn't have enough patience, you lost your temper, you spoke harshly. Given what your day was like, it's understandable that you had imperfect moments. Write out those moments in your journal, talk them out in your bereavement group, share with them with a trusted friend. Getting them out will help you forgive yourself for managing an often horrible situation the best you could.

I had a friend who shared with me the last few months of her brother's life. Young and dying of cancer, he received care from his parents and his wife and his siblings. Toward the end of his life, he wailed, "I just want someone to love me." My friend remembers the turmoil his cries caused, as family members did their best to share their love. My friend worried that her brother died believing he was unloved. What a difficult regret to keep.

Janet often visited Alan's grave to apologize to him. If that's not possible for you, she suggests writing a letter to your caree about your regrets. You can even pen a letter to yourself from your caree, imaging how your caree would respond to your apology. For instance, my friend could write a letter to her brother, sharing how much she wished he had died knowing he was loved. Then, she could write another letter, this time in her brother's voice, accepting the apology and letting her know he feels the love now and finds great comfort in the love of his family.

You may regret that you left your caree's bedside during his or her last moments which means your caree died alone and without you. During her last week, my Aunt Nancy received care in an inpatient hospice unit. As she died, her six children, their spouses and children as well my parents, my siblings and I held something like a vigil at her bedside. We prayed, recited psalms and spoke to her. Day after day, she held on. Until finally a hospice nurse suggested we leave the room and give Aunt Nancy time to herself. Soon after we left the room, Aunt Nancy died.

I believe death is a journey we travel with help from the family members and friends who've died before us. The energy of those still living can get in the way. We may say to our caree, "It's okay to go. We are all okay." And, yet, a caree can feel the love, which can lead to a struggle to leave. Often, we best help a caree accept the help that most helps (from those who've gone before us) when we physically remove ourselves from the room. You haven't failed if you miss the last moment. It's because you've been so successful that you can turn over the help to those most skilled in helping the final passage happen. It's the final act of letting go when you let family members who have already passed walk your caree to what's next.

I once gave a presentation to professionals who work in long-term settings about how family caregivers feel when they make the nursing home decision. After the presentation, an attendee approached me and said, "The worst day of my life was the day I placed my mother in a long-term care facility." That's a heavy regret to carry. Write the letter, visit the grave, talk it out with family and friends. Give the regrets a voice; when they remain silent they become toxic. When you talk out the regrets, you give yourself a chance to heal, to find the perspective, to understand the worst day was also probably your bravest.

As you work through your regrets, work into believing in a plan that's bigger than yours. Know that your caree is safe and happy and wishes the same for you. Your caree understands that death happens and that it was not your responsibility to prevent death. Most important, your caree wants you to have peace. Let go of regrets and embrace the peace.

You also may wonder about hope after your caree's death. The health care system can feed into your hope that your caree can continue, the diagnosis can be treated. And, no matter how realistic we are, we still hold onto hope. And, then death arrives. In a podcast, Anna Stookey, a therapist based in Beverly Hills, Calif., and I talked about where hope goes after a caree's death. We can feel hope betrayed us, which means we can feel bitter about this final outcome, this death.

As you wonder about hope, you also can't help but wonder about life after death. What happens after death? Where does the love go?

The energy you spent hoping during caregiving now needs to find another place, Anna explained. Anna shared an insight a client had after her father died. "I now look into a mirror and see him in me," the client said. "All his good qualities are inside me."

Know that hope is about living in, and making the most of, the present moment. The hope and love go to you—you hold the hope and the love because you understand how precious life is. You hold the possibilities of what was and will be. You understand that, because we can't control the outcome, we have to focus on making the most of what happens before the outcome. You are trusted to hold the hope and the love, which means you understand that the cycle of life requires letting go, over and over.

One of the greatest lessons you will learn because of your caree's death is the art of letting go. You cannot keep your caree in this life, you cannot time your caree's death, you can cannot control the length of time of your caree's life. You cannot control an outcome but only how you live in moments leading up to an outcome. And, that insight leads you to understand your life, which means you can let go of fears. You can let go while keeping hope and trust. Really, the only way to hold hope and trust and love is by letting go.

And, when you let go, you keep a compass in your life. Think of your caree, after death, as your life's greatest cheerleader. Your caree is well now. You can be, too. You are meant to be well.

In an interview with *CBS Sunday Morning*, Ally Breedlove spoke about coping with the loss of her younger brother, Ben, who died at 18 from a heart condition. "I can cope with missing him every day," she said, "because I believe he is more alive now than he has ever been."

In an Op/Ed piece entitled "In the Presence of All Souls" in *The New York Times*, T. M. Luhrmann writes that as "many as 80 percent of those who lose loved ones report that they sense that person after death."

In a blog post called "In Dreams," Robert Semenza, who cared for his wife, writes:

"After about two hours of tossing and turning, I suddenly saw my wife Marie lying quietly next to me. She looked so beautiful and so 'real' that I remember thinking that I was not dreaming, and even thought of rushing upstairs to get our son, Robert.

"I touched and kissed her face, which was as soft as it had always been, and asked her to open her eyes. I looked into those two 'dark olive pits,' which I would always tell her they looked like, and asked her if she had seen our family, and how they looked. She told me she had, and they were all 'young' and together. For some strange reason, I then asked her if one of my aunts was with her baby daughter, who had died as an infant, and she told me she was. She then told me how wonderful it was, and I replied that I would be there with them all some day. And she replied, 'How about tonight.' Typical Marie."

And, these comments from a member of The Beatles also may be words that comfort:

"At night when she came home she would cook, so we didn't have a lot of time with each other. But she was just a very comforting presence in my life. And when she died, one of the difficulties I had, as the years went by, was that I couldn't recall her face so easily. That's how it is for everyone, I think. As each day goes by, you just can't bring their face into your mind, you have to use photographs and reminders like that. So in this dream 12 years later, my mother appeared, and there was her face, completely clear, particularly her eyes, and she said to me very gently, very reassuringly: 'Let it be.'"
--Paul McCartney about his mom, who died when he was 14 and inspired the song "Let It Be," in an interview published by *The Telegraph*

Reconciling Resentments

The dichotomy of a death is that you may miss your caree at the same time as you resent his or her death. How could she leave you? How could he expect that you could continue? What in the world does she expect you to do now?

You may feel relief that caregiving has ended and then resent how much of your life it seemed to take.

You also may find that you resent others who have what you've lost—a spouse, a parent, a child, a life. You can't help but watch others who walk by with what you want (your spouse, your parent, your child, your sibling, your grandparent) and wonder why they have it but you don't.

And, certainly, you may regret family and friends who seemed to run at the first sign of caregiving. They went about their lives for as long as caregiving lasted for you. They don't have these struggles to start over, these fears that you've lost out, these anxieties about what's next. They seem to sleep at night while you still lie with one ear open, ready to help your caree who's no longer with you.

You may resent the government or a former employer or an institution for not providing you the financial support, help or choices you needed during caregiving which has left you in a desperate situation today. If only the government had paid you for taking care of your caree, then you wouldn't be in such deep debt. If only your former employer had benefits to help family caregivers, then you would have been able to continue working and you wouldn't be without a job right now. If only the home health agency had better caregivers, then you wouldn't have had to place your caree in a nursing home, which meant your inheritance was spent on care rather than available to you now when you really need it.

You resent your caree for leaving, others for living, family members for continuing, and society for not helping. You feel lost, adrift and alone. How do you find solid ground?

If you feel caregiving took too much of your life, holding resentments will take even more. Even worse, the resentments keep you in your past, begrudging an experience that is over. Move into today, decide to make the most of the moment you have now.

If you find yourself in a difficult circumstance, resenting the past will only keep you in your past. You won't find the solutions you need looking over your shoulder. You did the best you could. You made the best decisions available to you. There wasn't enough help for you during caregiving. However, you can get enough help today as you focus on solving the problems right in front of you.

Another way to remove resentments is to stop comparing. Let others live their lives while you give yourself a chance to live yours. When you resent others and their lives, you stop living yours. And, with all that you experienced and learned during caregiving, this is the time to take control of your life. It doesn't matter what life has done for them—it only matters what you'll do for your life.

Wrapping Up the Story

A friend recently shared the story of how another friend's mother died. The mother had suffered from heart disease and an addiction to pain medication during her last years. And, she truly suffered, which led to her constantly asking her children to assist her in committing suicide. Two sons immediately agreed to help but a daughter (my friend's friend) couldn't. Her mother's pleas lasted year after year until finally the daughter consented. With her children's help, the mother died peacefully.

The details of her mother's death now cause a bit of conflict for the daughter. How does she say her mom committed suicide without heading into a discussion she probably doesn't want?

The story of how your caree died may not be as difficult to tell as this one. But you may have parts of the story that you're not sure how to tell or if to tell. Perhaps other family members never showed up to say their "good-byes" to your caree. Perhaps another family member had a fight with the hospice nurse during your caree's last moments. Maybe your caree died in a hospital room when you so wished he had died at home. Maybe your caree died while you took a few minutes away for a bite to eat.

You can tell what works. For instance, the mother in the story above died peacefully with her family around her. And, she died after a long battle with heart disease. The daughter feels tremendous relief that her mother's suffering has ended. That's the story to tell: "My mother died peacefully and we all had a chance to say our good-byes. I'm so grateful her suffering has ended. Heart disease really took a toll on her."

As you struggle with a story, stick to successes. The difficult details can stay with you and remain separate from the story you tell others. What's most important is to tell the aspects that comfort you. Perhaps you were grateful to be holding hands with your caree at the end, or touched by how many wanted to be with your caree before he or she died, or sad at how much you miss your caree, or comforted by the hospice staff who so lovingly cared for your caree, or at peace because your caree died surrounded by flowers and sunshine in her room. Share the successes of your story because that's the important story to tell.

Working Out Worries

Will I ever feel better? Will the grieving end? Will I be able to go out by myself? Will I be able to celebrate holidays? Will the family stay intact? Will I ever be needed again? Am I too far behind to ever get caught up?

Janet Cromer had a friend who told her, "The sweetness will come back into life." Not this day, maybe not the next day and maybe not until next year but life will get better for you. Cope with your pain; don't judge it or minimize it or dramatize it.

Think about how you managed your stresses and challenges during caregiving. What got you to the next day? What got you to this day? You have an ability to survive and this ability will help you now. Chances are, you learned to take life minute by minute. This is a great coping strategy right now especially because some moments you'll feel okay and others you won't.

If you feel good in the moment when someone invites you to a function, then feel horrible during the function, that's okay. If you feel good today and awful tomorrow, know that bad days will some day be fewer and farther in between. Commit to enjoying the good days and managing the bad days. When you've got a good day, take advantage of it. When you've hit a bad day, manage it rather than resisting it.

You may have worries about whether or not your family will stay intact in the future. Michelle Norman, who cared for her parents, worked closely with one of her brothers to provide care. A sister lived out of town and another lived in town but mostly in denial. Another brother did what he could. Her parents died within months of each other. Michelle wanted her brothers and sisters to attend holidays and family functions after their parents' death because remaining a family meant the world to her. She worried so much about what would happen to the core of her parents' family—their children and her siblings.

During the first year after Michelle's parents died, Michelle's daughter celebrated her first birthday. It was a difficult time for Michelle—celebrating her daughter's birthday and really missing her parents. Worse, her sister did not attend the birthday party. After more unsuccessful attempts to bring the family together, Michelle finally released herself from the responsibility of keeping the family together. When she let go of the worry, she also took the pressure off herself of inviting everyone to all family events. Instead, she now focuses on including those she knows want to be in the fold. Her brother who helped during caregiving became the family member she could depend on and that became enough for her. The relief that came with the decision surprised her. She had a few moments of guilt about the decision and then decided to enjoy how much happier the decision makes her.

It's hard to understand how some family members can be right there with you and others can't. If others pull away, keep them in your heart. Resist the temptation to hold a grudge because you can't know the future. You can't know if they will come back. If they come back, you'll be so glad you kept them in your heart while they were gone.

Because you may worry that caregiving took your time, you may think you must move through all this as quickly as possible. So, as you worry you don't have enough, I will remind you to take your time. Your family, your day, your life will look different to you. You're settling into new, which takes time. Rather than rush it, experience it.

Think of your worries as a call to action. As you work through your worries, write them out. Then, make a plan for each worry. Who can help? What can help? What can you change that can help? What resource can you use that can help? What choice can you make that will help? Karol Ward's book, *Worried Sick*, has helpful exercises you can use to help you work through the worries.

You may worry that life forgot you or left you behind. I can guarantee you that your life remembers you. It's waiting for you because your life knows all you can do. It just witnessed you manage a horribly stressful, heartbreaking time. Life understands all that you can accomplish. It's ready for you. Let's open up your life.

~ Open ~

"Vulnerability is the only authentic state. Being vulnerable means being open for wounding but also for pleasure. Being open to the wounds of life means also being open to the bounty and beauty. Don't mask or deny your vulnerability: it is your greatest asset. Be vulnerable: quake and shake in your boots with it. The new goodness that is coming to you in the form of people, situations, and things can only come to you when you are vulnerable, i.e., open." ~ Stephen Russell, author of Barefoot Doctor's Guide to the Tao: A Spiritual Handbook for the Urban Warrior

Annie Dillard said it best: How we spend our days is, of course, how we spend our lives.

Caregiving felt like the world got smaller. In your life after caregiving, the world will seem too big. You'll look out into the rest of your life and see a vast void or an overwhelming chaos. Either way, it looks awful.

The rest of your life is simply about today. Focus on each day. And, when the day feels like forever, focus on parts of your day—the morning, then lunch, then dinner, then evening, then bedtime.

You may feel awful about the fact that you are starting over. It can feel like you are the only who must begin again. And, you may feel like you are the only one starting over at your age. Know that starting over is one of the over-looked life skills. We start over all the time, each day, actually. Starting over is not about your failure but about life moving you into next. And, it's not really starting over. It's about picking up where you are, in this exact place and time, and choosing to be open to next.

Outing Grief

Your grief may feel like a pain that can't stop. Get help for your grief. Join a support group, write in your journal, see a counselor. A friend who lost his daughter shared this perspective on time: Time does heal. It matters, though, how you use the time.

You may feel that you manged your grief well enough during caregiving that you are ready to move into the next phase of life. I met Tom, who cared for his wife, at a presentation I gave called "What's Love Got to Do with It?" The presentation was about staying in love during caregiving, illness and dementia. Tom thought the presentation was about dating after loss. He arrived early to the presentation ready to find out what he needed. "I'm dating for the first time in 59 years," he said. "I just want to make sure I know what to expect." I met Tom in May; his wife had died in February. Now, you may say, Well, that's how a man approaches grief.

Consider Heather Campbell Furtek Slutzky, who cared for her husband. During the first year after his death, Heather completely changed her life—she moved to a different state and changed careers.

Karen Gurney, who cared for her mother and brother, found that she needed to take care of her grief separate from her family members. "When my brother died and again when my mother died, even though my siblings came to help, I was in charge of all of the arrangements," she said. "I really did not have the opportunity to express my grief at that time as much as I needed to. I needed to be strong for others."

Three months after her mother's funeral, Karen's local hospital invited her to attend an ecumenical ceremony for those grieving a family member or friend who recently died. "(This) was such a valuable, healing experience for me," Karen said. "I thought about not going. Then I thought I would go to support others. I found that others supported me. We were able to share stories of our loved ones and of our loss. I didn't need to be strong. I cried a lot and so did others. We spontaneously reached out to each other. The two pastors who conducted the service stayed on and talked to us individually. I wish that everyone who has lost a loved one could have such an experience."

Everyone handles grief differently. You can read about it and talk about it and then decide what feels right for you. You get to make the rules. And, because it's your experience, you are the one who has to understand it. If others want you to move on, to be over it, and you simply can't, then spend time instead with those who understand what it's really like.

And, that means that some days you'll want to go out and some days you won't. You may be able to manage some social functions without tears and some you may not. What you could mange yesterday may feel impossible today. Grief can't be tamed. So it becomes about coping.

Because you may feel okay until you don't and when you don't feel okay may be when you're out, develop an explanation you can use when you need it. For instance, you're at the movies with a friend and for some reason you just miss your caree more than ever. The tears start no matter how much you want them to stop. You can simply say, "I am having a bad moment right now. I'm going to the bathroom for a few moments. I will be back."

When you return—after 10 minutes or one hour—simply say, "Thank you so much for understanding. I appreciate that so much." You don't have to apologize because you can't apologize for grief.

Your Day

When you wake up in the morning, you may think, "I can't do this. I can't get up and I can't face it." It can feel overwhelming to open your day.

It also can feel like too difficult to look into a day that feels too empty. You may be tempted to fill your day with your past. Beth, one of my coaching clients, cared for her mother at home until her mother's death. During caregiving, she turned her home's living room and dining room into a suite for her mom, adding plumbing in the dining room for a sink and toilet. After her mom's death, after the medical equipment supplier came to pick up the hospital bed that filled the dining room, Beth moved her home office into the dining room. Each day, she sat in the room that was neither a dining room or a bathroom or an office. It was the past.

Beth paid the house's mortgage with help from her mother and knew that after her mother's death she would have to sell the home. So, on a regular basis, a Realtor would show the home, walking prospective buyers into two rooms—the living room and dining room/bathroom/office—that seemed to house a dead person. Only after a coaching session which helped her see that keeping the toilet in the dining room kept her family in the past and closer to financial difficulties did Beth remove the sink and toilet and turn the room back into a dining room. Once she did that, the house sold and her family moved into a house they could afford.

Martha, who cared for her mom, was a member of one of my online support groups. We recently touched base and began to reminisce about the members of our group. She shared an update about one member, Linda, who also cared for her mom. Once in awhile, Linda will reach out to Martha with the same message: "How do I go on? I can't go on without my mom. How do you do it?" Martha's answer remains the same: You can't live in the past.

The toughest part of your day may be those moments when you wake up but don't want to get up. Get up and have breakfast. Use the night before to prepare the next morning's breakfast. Set the table, put the coffee maker on a timer so it's ready for you, have your favorite cereal at the ready. Tell yourself that's all you have to do—just get up and have breakfast.

During caregiving, bad habits may have helped you survive the day. Now, though, you may think these bad habits (biting your nails, zoning out in front of the TV, eating as fast as you can) may also be what keeps you in your past.

As you can, look to turn the bad habits into good habits. For instance, rather than biting your nails, give yourself a weekly manicure. Rather than zoning out in front the of the TV, try to get lost in a good book. And, before sitting down to a meal, set a timer for 30 minutes to remind yourself you have time to enjoy the meal.

You can go one step further as you create these good habits by turning them into treasured rituals. Think of rituals as adding a ceremonial touch to the ordinary which transforms the ordinary into special. So, for instance, you add an ambiance around the weekly manicure you give yourself at home—you light candles, play your favorite music, sit in your favorite room.

Let's say you love to go to the library every week. Schedule a regular day and time for a weekly trip to the library. Before going to the library, read online reviews of books, making notes that you'll bring with you to the library. Once you arrive at the library, stop to say "Hello" to your favorite librarian and then stroll through the rows of books as you select the ones you want. After leaving the library, stop at your favorite coffee house so you can start to read one of the books right away.

You can create a ritual around your meals. At dinner time, set the table with flowers and a tablecloth and your best plates (or your best paper plates), light a candle, play your favorite music. Or, perhaps you invite friends, neighbors, family members, other former family caregivers to join you for dinner. If you have out-of-town friends, perhaps ask them to Skype with you at dinner time so you can enjoy a meal together virtually.

You also can create rituals to help you start and end the day. Look to create a ritual that happens after breakfast that brings comfort to you. The ritual could be writing in your journal or sending a text to a friend or watching the sun rise. Allow the ritual to prop you up and into your day. At the end of the day, a ritual could help you relax a bit, which again could be writing in your journal, writing down three gratitudes, taking the dog for one last walk.

Rituals will be helpful when you have days that double as anniversaries and holidays. You can use these rituals to bring you extra comfort during these tough days. You also can build on these rituals to add new rituals to holidays and specials days that you shared with your caree. As you navigate the holidays after your caree's death, be open to honoring your caree and changing up the traditions if you feel better with a change. Again, the rituals are about being fully present in your life today as you honor the past. Be open to the suggestions and ideas of other family members as you talk out what you need.

You may simply dread these days whether they are part of a celebration others enjoy (like Thanksgiving) or just a day that represents special importance to you (like the first day of hospice care). You may find that anticipating the anniversaries and holidays is much worse than the actual day. So, you'll want to create two plans--one for managing your anticipation and one to cope with the actual day.
A plan to manage the anticipation could be that you write out what you dread about the day —the get-together itself, missing your caree, the change in tradition because you caree is no longer here. You may dread going alone or dread feeling alone. Nothing that you dread is silly so don't dismiss or minimize. Another plan could be talking it out with your bereavement group—asking them how they manage the anticipation, what they dread, which anniversary or holiday feels the most difficult.

A plan to manage the day could include a back-up plan if you're having a difficult day and must leave a get-together, or a statement you use when you're struggling, or an individual you decide you'll sit with at dinner. If it's a day that you will spend alone, perhaps you plan how you'll spend the morning or evening in memory of your caree. Perhaps you decide to volunteer to help others in your community, giving you a healing purpose and an engaging activity.

With each plan that manages the anticipation and the day, bring in the memory of your caree, including your favorite stories. Your memories mean you share the day with your caree. Be open with other family members and friends about how much comfort you receive when you share these memories. If others feel uncomfortable as you share your memories, know you can share memories in other ways—your journal, your blog, your support group.

During the days after caregiving, you may feel you are at your worst but still required to participate in your life. You may have to work or have family or a spouse who count on you. How can you deliver, you may think, when you simply feel lost.

Know that loss hurts, which means you will need regular chances to heal. Healing means tears, sadness and heartache. Healing also means being vulnerable, which feels like a weakness but is actually a strength. Your vulnerability will become your greatest asset because it connects you to support and solutions. When you're vulnerable, you can take the next step to solve the hurt. When you resist vulnerability, you stay stuck in pain. Talk about your hurt with others who understand or write it out so that it no longer weighs heavy on your heart. Make your healing a priority.

These tips can help you be your best during the worst:

1. Find a safe place to be your worst.
The strong remain strong because they give themselves a chance to feel the pain, to cry the tears, to miss a loved one. Allow yourself time to cry and grieve—and when you do, accept those moments of crying and missing as a blessing. You are giving yourself a chance to heal.

2. Track good news.
You may be caught up in counting how long it's been since your caree died. Try to also tally good news: How many walks you've taken in a week, how often you've written in your journal, how many times you've smiled at a stranger. Tracking the good news will help you see that life can be good again. To help you, I've included "I'm Okay" worksheets in our Resources section. These worksheets help guide you through the first eight weeks after caregiving ends.

3. Listen to where your story gets stuck.
We all tell a story about our lives. And, the story we tell broadcasts much about how we feel, think and act within our life. The story we tell often becomes the life we live. We all have woe-is-me days (and sometimes weeks). Woe-is-me feels good initially; we can go to a corner and lick our wounds. But perpetual woe-is-me means we stay in the corner; our self-pity keeps us cowering, unable to take steps or consider solutions which could make us feel better.

A story stuck in self-pity could sound like this: "My husband died and here I am, all alone. He took everything with him when he died and left me nothing."

A story that speaks honestly about life after caregiving could sound like this: "My husband died a few months ago. I miss him so much. I am doing my best to make the most of each day."

In the first story, the former family caregiver has nothing. In this second story, the former family caregiver has her best.

Listen to the stories you tell about your life and your experiences. What do the stories give to you? Do they give you a second chance, an opportunity to heal, self-respect? Or do the stories take from you? You get to tell the story of your life—choose the version that helps you stand tall.

4. Enjoy beauty regularly.
Life can feel so painful. And, yet our world contains so much beauty. We can look out our window and see beauty. We can open up a book and read beauty. We can attend a concert and hear beauty. During a difficult period in my life, I watched an episode of a favorite television show (*Mad Men*). At the end of the episode, I thought: What a beautiful episode—the writing, the costumes, the direction, the acting. And then's when I thought: We are given the gift of beauty to offset the price of pain. You have pain in your life but you also have beauty in your day. See it. Read it. Hear it. Taste it. Beauty surrounds you at all times, especially during a time of pain.

5. Take time to look good.
You may think, "Who cares how I look?" You care. Giving time to your clothes and your appearance means you respect who you are and who you can be.

6. Go outside.
Even on days when you don't think you can face the world, step outside. Sit outside. Nature can heal.

7. Borrow someone else's hope.
When it all ends, you may feel that your hope has reached its dead end. You may struggle to understand how to hope again. You may think you can't find hope for your next phase in life. Take a page from the book of someone who has lost and overcome. Read autobiographies, rent movies which showcase how others make it through difficulties and how they rediscover their hope. And, then borrow their hope. Know because they did you can, too.

8. Give yourself time to respond.
You may hear suggestions, advice, opinions. You also may feel that you need to immediately respond, which leaves you feeling flummoxed and tongue-tied. Your response can be, "I'll think about that." You can think about it (the suggestion, advise or opinion) and discard, act on it or revise it. Know you have time to respond and that you can choose what's right for you. If an individual follows up to check if you took the suggestion, followed the advice, decided her opinion was right, you can say, "I appreciate your concern. I'm going in a different direction. I'm so grateful for all the support I have right now."

9. Create.
You're in a place of pain. Creativity can be one of the ways you work through the pain. Write, paint, draw, color, crochet, knit, garden, build. Through your hands, you can make and release.

10. Slow down your decisions.
You may feel the panic of deciding right now what needs to happen. Slowing down a decision can simply mean you sleep on it. Or, it means, you mull it over for a week. Or, it can be that you table the decision until next year.

11. Find your perspective.
It's a tough time for you. A helpful perspective may be, "This too shall pass." Or, "I am one of many struggling and suffering right now. I am not alone in my pain." Or, you may realize

that the loss of your caree is difficult but the blessing is that you know so much more about your caree than other family members. Find a perspective that honors you and your past while opening up possibilities for you in your future.

12. Clear your clutter.
The clutter could be mail you haven't opened or tasks you've been putting off. The clutter could be toxic relationships that seem to suck the life out of you. The clutter could be a decision you're putting off because of a fear. Schedule time each week—even just a few moments—to clear your clutter. If you're pushing something back into the drawer and then avoiding the drawer, you've got clutter that needs your attention.

13. Arrive everywhere loved.
Ron Gladis, a family caregiver for his wife, shared this insight from his wife with me: "Arrive everywhere loved." Arrive into your day loved. A tough time becomes tougher if we feel we must earn or win the love of others in our lives. You are loved. Begin each day with the profound and confident belief that you are loved. That confidence will attract more love to you.

14. Let go of controlling how others feel about your situation.
Some people will be on board with you. Others won't. Focus on those who support you. Let go of those who don't. And, let go of the idea that you must convince those who don't support you that you are right. That will easily turn into a battle that will end with you feeling like you lost a war. It's okay that others disagree with your decisions and actions. Just make sure you feel good about them.

15. Choose kindness.
When we're in pain, it can be so easy to lash out in pain and cause others pain. As hard as it can be, choose kindness. Be kind to others—when you agree with them, when you disagree with them, when you decide they are not a good fit for you. And, most important, be kind with yourself.

16. Decide what's best for you.
During caregiving, you often made decisions based on what was best for your caree. Now, decide what's best for you. Say "No" without guilt when a situation or relationship or opportunity isn't right for you. What's best for you is best.

16. Remember there's a time and a place for your worst; show others your best.
When you go out in the world, you will face others' good news. As you struggle, family members and friends will have weddings, babies, promotions, vacations. You may feel as if you've been robbed of any good news. The challenge is to celebrate when others have joy. Even if you feel you've been robbed, it's important not to rob another. When someone shares good news, envision yourself in their good news, feel how it feels to have such good news. It's magical when good happens. Feel that magic and then extend your good wishes and congratulations. When you do, you buy yourself some magic.
You're at your best when you try. You're at your best when you say, "I've tried but this isn't right for me." You're at your best when you protect yourself with limits and boundaries. No matter how deep the grief, you can be your best simply by embracing compassion for yourself.

Your Routine

I like the idea of a routine because it can keep us moving. You wake at a certain time, you eat breakfast at a certain time, you go to work at the same time. You may feel that certain times of the day are the worst—the times that you enjoyed most with your caree or that hold the greatest memory of your caree. You may dread these times of the day. Work these times into your routine; these times are your time to remember your caree. If you resist these times because they feel too painful, you don't give yourself a chance to move past the pain.

You might try "replacement therapy," an idea created by Donna Webb, who cared for her mother. In a blog post she wrote on CareGiving.com, Donna explained, "I am looking for ideas of what to do to replace all the things I have done for Mom these past years, to fill those time slots with instructive, creative, supportive alternatives. Remember, there are emotional connections worked in there, habits of doing specific things at specific times (and) restrictions of freedom that have to be broken through."

I suggested to Donna the following:

1. Write down the schedule (time and task) of caregiving responsibilities for your mom.

2. Once you have your list, write down one thing you enjoyed about each task with your mom.

3. Then, use this list of enjoyments to begin to recreate your day: Replace the caregiving activity with an activity that creates a similar experience or emotion or enjoyment for you. Perhaps during the time when feeding your mom took place, you now bake or write down your mom's favorite recipes. And, perhaps when you provided personal care, you now use that time to create with your hands.

4. I would also say that, for now, build in some quiet time. During the quiet time, contemplate: How will you use free time when you have it? How will you bring your caregiving knowledge to the community? Who will you be when you go out as a "Godspeed Caregiver"? What would your mom wish for you during this next stage of life?

5. Finally, this transitioning will be bumpy. Feel the bumps, take time to readjust. The bumps can be a great guide because they may nudge you to see a possibility you may have ignored.

Let's use the idea of replacement therapy for Sam, who cared for his father. He dreaded the afternoon hours because he and his father spent the afternoon watching movies. He missed his father's companionship. In the afternoon, Sam craves companionship. His replacement therapy could be taking the dog for a walk, volunteering at the local nursing home, tutoring children after school.

We can't talk about your day without acknowledging that your nights may make your days feel like a cake walk. Janet Cromer, who cared for her husband, struggled to sleep for a year after her husband's death. She worried she would miss something during the night because she became so used to waking at night to help her husband, Alan. Training her body to not be at the ready, to instead relax, became a significant challenge. She missed her husband. She was used to being on call. To help overcome the pain and the anxiousness, she meditated, did yoga and stretched to reverse the stress response. She also spoke to herself, "It is okay to be lonely. It won't always be this bad. I may have a good dream tonight, I don't have to be afraid."

It look a year for Janet to sleep again through the night. Her patience can inspire you to be patient with your transitions, too.

Your Health

Because you hurt, you may feel like ice cream, Doritos, Big Macs and M&Ms will help you feel better. Know that when you reach for the Ben & Jerry's, you're really reaching for comfort. Comfort food once in awhile will taste perfect. Too much, though, and you'll simply feel awful.

Work to replace a comfort food with a healing food—carrots for potato chips, grapes for candy, for instance. Start by deciding to add one healthy food option into your day (like a healthy afternoon snack) and then build from there.

You may feel like you've gained weight since caregiving ended. The constant motion required in caregiving may have kept the weight off. Now, you seem to be spend more time sitting. Do your best to take a walk every day. The walk will help you manage stress and worries, add a purpose in your day and help keep the weight off.

Rather than reaching for candy, maybe you reach for the credit card. Caregiving can feel like the desert—you never had enough—so now you want to fill up with enough. So, you shop and shop and buy and buy. A little retail therapy can do a world of good. A lot can lead you to the poor house. Before your purchase, ask yourself, "What do I really want to buy?" If you really want the possession or the trip and it fits in the budget, then make the buy. If you're really hoping to buy away the blues or the fear of what's next, or avoid what feels empty, then talk with your support group or a therapist. Money is a tool to live a comfortable life—it's not the cure for your life.

You may feel that caregiving left you bloodied and bruised, that your body really took a hit because of caregiving. Your back may hurt from the grueling transfers and personal care, your shoulder may hurt from lifting and transferring your caree. Just as your soul needs time to heal, know your body will need time, too.

Schedule a doctor's appointment so you have an understanding of your current health. You may drag your feet because it's been so long you can't even imagine that the appointment will be anything but bad news. Go. The information that you receive about your health will help you take control of your health. If you continue to wait, you'll lose control. If you are worried about the costs of an appointment, check with the Health Resources and Services Administration of U.S. Department of Health and Human Services about free and low-cost clinics in your area.

You also may wonder about your emotional health. Are you grieving or is it depression? How do you know if you need help from professionals?
According to the Centers for Disease Control, the signs of depression include:

- Feelings of hopelessness and/or pessimism
- Feelings of guilt, worthlessness, and/or helplessness
- Irritability, restlessness
- Loss of interest in activities or hobbies once pleasurable
- Fatigue and decreased energy
- Difficulty concentrating, remembering details, and making decisions

- Insomnia, early-morning wakefulness, or excessive sleeping
- Overeating, or appetite loss
- Thoughts of suicide, suicide attempts
- Persistent aches or pains, headaches, cramps, or digestive problems that do not get better, even with treatment

If you experience any of these symptoms, speak with your doctor about your symptoms and ask for a referral to a therapist. If you work and your employer has an Employee Assistance Program, call the EAP for a referral to a counselor. You also can speak with your minister or priest or rabbi. If you used hospice services, check with hospice about bereavement benefits available to you. Please don't make the decision to simply live with your depression. Depression, like any diagnosis, needs a treatment plan. When you have a treatment plan for your depression, you give yourself better days.

If you feel your grief deepens over time, you may be suffering from complicated grief, "an intense and long-lasting form of grief that takes over your life," according to The Center for Complicated Grief. The organization says you may be suffering from complicated grief if you have many of these symptoms for more than six months after the death of your caree:

- Strong feelings of yearning or longing for the person who died
- Feeling intensely lonely, even when other people are around
- Strong feelings of anger or bitterness related to the death
- Feeling like life is empty or meaningless without the person who died
- Thinking so much about the person who died that it interferes with doing things or with relationships with other people
- Strong feelings of disbelief about the death or finding it very difficult to accept the death
- Feeling shocked, stunned, dazed or emotionally numb
- Finding it hard to care about or to trust other people
- Feeling very emotionally or physically activated when confronted with reminders of the loss
- Avoiding people, places, or things that are reminders of the loss
- Strong urges to see, touch, hear, or smell things to feel close to the person who died

If you feel you may be experiencing complicated grief, contact The Center for Complicated Grief (www.complicatedgrief.org) for a referral to a therapist.

During your caregiving experience, you may have experienced a trauma. You may have seen your caree's stroke or car accident. The last months of your caree's life may have included suffering which caused too much suffering for you to bear. You may have witnessed medical interventions that simply shocked.

The trauma may result in Post-Traumatic Stress Disorder. According to National Institute for Mental Health, "PTSD develops after a terrifying ordeal that involved physical harm or the threat of physical harm. The person who develops PTSD may have been the one who was harmed, the harm may have happened to a loved one, or the person may have witnessed a harmful event that happened to loved ones or strangers."

The Institute groups the symptoms of PTSD into the following three categories:

1. Re-experiencing symptoms
- Flashbacks—reliving the trauma over and over, including physical symptoms like a racing heart or sweating
- Bad dreams
- Frightening thoughts.
- Re-experiencing symptoms may cause problems in a person's everyday routine. They can start from the person's own thoughts and feelings. Words, objects, or situations that are reminders of the event can also trigger re-experiencing.

2. Avoidance symptoms
- Staying away from places, events, or objects that are reminders of the experience
- Feeling emotionally numb
- Feeling strong guilt, depression, or worry
- Losing interest in activities that were enjoyable in the past
- Having trouble remembering the dangerous event.

Things that remind a person of the traumatic event can trigger avoidance symptoms. These symptoms may cause a person to change his or her personal routine. For example, after a bad car accident, a person who usually drives may avoid driving or riding in a car.

3. Hyperarousal symptoms
- Being easily startled
- Feeling tense or "on edge"
- Having difficulty sleeping, and/or having angry outbursts.

Hyperarousal symptoms are usually constant instead of being triggered by things that remind one of the traumatic event. They can make the person feel stressed and angry. These symptoms may make it hard to do daily tasks, such as sleeping, eating or concentrating.

If you think you may be suffering from PTSD, contact a therapist or counselor for help. The therapist or counselor can help you work through the trauma and suggest treatments to help.

Your Family and Friends

Many family and friends may have disappeared during caregiving. Or, perhaps now, after caregiving, they seem to just be greedy, insensitive nuts. I love this advice dispensed by Dr. Phil several years ago on his TV show. He said he has family members who are idiots. He copes with them by loving them through their difficult moments. You may feel that you have to love family members through their difficult decades. You also may feel it's best to love them from afar. Loving them from a distance through their difficult moments is forgiveness.

You also may think: I can't get past the hate to get to the love. I do think we have to feel the deep pain before we can embrace forgiveness. You've been hurt—how could you not feel intensely about a family member or friend? My suggestion about hating is to hate privately, letting out your feelings to a trusted confidant, your journal, your dog. Publicly declaring your issues with a family member or friend, especially on social media, only makes the matters worse. I've found that silence dulls the animosity. Meaning, when you don't engage, the battle can't continue. Most important, hate in the short term, love in the long term.

A fellow life coach shared a technique he used when he had to learn to deal with a very difficult daughter-in-law. Their son had divorced his wife but she stayed in their lives because of their grandchildren. The life coach and his wife wanted to have the best relationship possible with the daughter-in-law because of their concern and love for their grandchildren.

So, the life coach and his wife created three wishes for their daughter-in-law that they said every day. Here's how he did it: He thought about what he wished for himself. Let's say he wanted peace, abundance and joy in his life. So, each day, he would say to himself, "I wish peace, abundance and joy for Daughter-in-Law." The wishes for her took him out of the anger and anguish and into a place of graciousness.

You can do the same. You can turn your wishes into prayers or meditations. Whatever you wish for yourself, wish for the family members who cause you pain. You'll ease your own pain in the process. When you move out of pain, you move into better—better relationships, better days, a better life.

You also may have been the friend or family member who disappeared simply because caregiving encompassed your life. You may have regularly canceled on friends and family members. You may have missed important events. You may feel like you have to re-create relationships which somehow changed without you.

Know you can become a part of these relationships again. Ask for forgiveness from those who may have become less of a priority for you during caregiving. You may feel shame about this and be tempted to be silent and withdrawn. Own the situation—that you want to reconnect, that you apologize for being amiss. Be the friend or parent or adult child or sibling that you want to be. Be present, be a good listener, be compassionate, be forgiving, be open. You don't want to continue to miss out in these relationships. That, truly, would be the worst thing you can do.

You may still be in a caregiving situation, perhaps caring for the other parent, or looking at another caregiving situation on the horizon. Be sure to keep room for grieving as you continue to care. Janice Goldsborough, who lost her father and still helps her mother, spoke with me during a podcast about grieving while caregiving. She said the best decision she made was to see a counselor for her grief. Her therapist simply let her cry during her sessions—which is what she needed to do but didn't feel she could do in front of her mother and her two teen-aged daughters.

Janice also spoke with her daughters about her grief and how much she missed their grandfather. The temptation is to shield difficulties from children. Instead, show them how to manage the difficulties and loss. Encourage discussions about how they feel about their loss, their memories of your caree, what they miss about your caree. Keep them involved in decisions about changes to holiday traditions and rituals. Involve them in your creative pursuits and take long walks with them. Be a trusted, honest presence for them.

If a caregiving situation continues (or dances in front of you), you may be tempted to think you must continue to put your life on hold. On the contrary, continue into the next phase of your life. Keep going, taking caregiving with you.

Socializing

During caregiving, your world revolved around illness and decline. Then after caregiving ends, you realize the world also includes activities and events and, well, life. You may wonder how you fit into this life that feels so wonderfully busy and yet so uncomfortably odd. The world looks so scary and yet so interesting. You'd like to be in that world except you wonder how to step into it, how to get your footing.

You also may wonder how you'll be able to be out in the world without your caree. You may miss the physical presence of your caree. You also may miss the check-ins required when you went out during caregiving. During caregiving, you may have hated your cell phone because it always rang with bad news. Now, you may wish for it—it feels like it was your connection to purpose, to meaning, to you.

You may struggle with how you feel about socializing. You may feel like the third wheel—with other friends, with your children, alone in a coffee shop. Or, you may feel that laughing and enjoying life after a loss disrespects your caree.

Life is for the living. Enjoy your life as often and as soon as you can. Enjoying your life is how you respect your caree. The greatest challenge during caregiving was learning how to keep your life. Now, you may struggle with how to live your life. One step at a time, go out. If you don't enjoy yourself or don't feel like the venue or company is right for you, then you can make a different decision about these invitations in the future.

Before you go out, have some simple statements ready to use when you're not ready to share too much about your life or when you're ready to leave before the event is over.

The simple statements could be:

"My spouse recently died. I'm adjusting right now both to missing him/her and to this new life. I'm glad to be here because it puts me back into life. I hope you don't mind if I ask you for some suggestions on how to navigate this."

"I'm glad to be here. I'm feeling a bit awkward as I was home so long when I cared for my mom. So bear with me."

"I must go. I'm so thankful you invited me tonight. I enjoyed meeting and sharing with everyone."

"I'm having a difficult day today so I'm going to go home early. I am okay. I can send you a text when I get home."

If you are feeling unsure or unsettled or awkward during an event, simply go to the bathroom. Give yourself a minute to gather your thoughts. Think about what you need. Do you need an introduction to someone at the party so you're not standing alone? Ask the hostess to introduce you to the nicest person at the party. Do you need to leave? Then, decide it's time for your exit and then be ready with your good-bye, which could be: "I loved being here tonight. Thank you so much for inviting me. I'm going to get my coat and head home. I will call you tomorrow to find out what I missed."

You may worry about unexpected tears. Whatever you say or do, you are doing your best. It's okay. You may be hurt by insensitive comments by others. A friend who cared for her husband shared a comment a friend made to her a few months after her husband's death. "Do you still miss him?" the friend asked. My friend understood what her friend meant to ask ("What do you miss about him?) but couldn't help but feel hurt by the friend's comment, which came across as rather insensitive. My friend also found that some wanted her to feel better after a certain time—like one year later—and couldn't quite get that it still hurt. And, for my friend, the second year posed challenges for her simply because, well, her husband, her love, was still gone.

People simply won't know what to say or do. And, you may not be able to tell them what to say or do. You're all taking steps into unknown territory, which means there will be missteps. If someone hurts your feelings, you can say, "Oh, gosh, that stung." Do your best to share why it hurt and what you need. If a friend or family member can't help your healing, then move on to those who can.

You may dread running errands because you may dread who will you will see. You may dread the grocery store because you no longer need to buy your caree's favorite foods. You may dread going to church because it feels like everyone watches to see how you're doing.

You may hesitate to socialize because you won't know how to answer questions that once seemed so simple but now seem horribly complex. You can answer questions truthfully and with little detail. I have a friend who's first-born died shorty after birth. We were once at a gathering that included friends of friends—people we didn't know. I listened as a new acquaintance asked how many children he had. He answered, in one of the kindness voices I've ever heard, "We have four children, two girls and a boy and a little one who died shortly after birth." His response was so lovely—it honored his family as it remembered a loss. His answer didn't demand anything from his listeners and yet allowed us to connect with him on a very personal level. His story, his truth, became a gift I felt I received.

You will need time and practice to find your story. Start with your truth: "My (mother, brother, grandparent) recently died. I'm still raw so I may be a little emotional." You don't have to withhold or hide a fact to try to make another comfortable.

You may encounter people who seem to have forgotten about your caree's death. As they engage you in small talk, they may ask after your caree. You can simply respond, "My (mother, brother, daughter) died a few months ago. Thank you so much for asking about her." If they ask about your caree and then turn bright red after remembering your caree has died, you can say, "It's okay. Some days, she feels very much alive to me. I appreciate you asking about her."

Give yourself permission to fumble and hide and stammer. Give yourself as much time as you need to figure out what to say and how to say it. And, if you say it with tears, well, that's how you say it. You don't have to make others comfortable and you don't have to worry about how others feel about your emotions. If you lose your temper, call later and apologize. As my friend does with his story, you just have to give yourself the truth of each moment and what the truth of each moment feels like. When you feel better, it will be better.

Simply take care of the situation by taking care of yourself. When your body tells you it needs your care, listen and act.

Coping with Loss

You may have lost your caree but you also may feel you have lost yourself. The losses you feel after caregiving ends may feel like boxes piled on top of boxes always in front of you. You can't get around the losses.

Label those boxes. Meaning, name what you've lost: Your caree, your caregiving role, your expectation of your future, your financial stability, your dreams, your sense of humor, your ability to give, your best friend, your purpose, yourself. You just may feel so spent during caregiving that you can't even begin to think about caring or giving again.

Try this exercise to help you work though your losses. Take a shoe box and a stack of sticky notes. On a sticky note, write out a loss. Then, stick the note on the shoe box. Now, fill the shoe box with all that's related to that loss. For example, you've lost your best friend. Write that on a sticky note that you stick on the box. The impact of losing your best friend is:

- No one gets your jokes.
- You go out to eat alone.
- You don't have anyone to call on those bad days.
- You miss him.

Each side effect of the loss becomes a sticky note that you place in the shoe box. Keep filling the shoe box, which may take 10 minutes or 10 days. Feel the pain of the losses, acknowledge the emptiness.

When you're ready, empty the shoe box. You have choices as to what to do with those notes that represent your losses. You can recycle the sticky notes, tuck them away in an envelope, or burn them. You may want to save them for a few days and then shred them. You choose how to manage the losses.

You may feel like all these losses leave you feeling empty. You may fear the emptiness, that you'll spend the rest of life without. Know the emptiness is part of your transition to being full again. The transition will not happen overnight but it will happen. You will cross the bridge from empty to full.

You can take a step toward crossing the bridge when you can make the losses your gains. As you look at these notes that contain your losses, think about how you want to let go of the losses so you can find your gains.

When you're ready, flip the loss. Let's stay with the example of losing your best friend. Look at the loss from the perspective of a gain. Ask yourself: What did your best friend leave you?

Your answers may be:

- Amazing memories.
- The skills I need to cherish and nurture friendships.
- His favorite sweatshirt.
- His love of life.

Now, write "Because of my best friend, I have" on a sticky note which you place on the shoe box. Then make up sticky for each gain, filling the box with those sticky notes. When you're done, go through the sticky notes. Keep the ones that you just love and stick them around the house, on mirrors, walls, cabinets. Maybe you place "I have amazing memories" on your bathroom mirror. "I have his love of life" gets stuck on the refrigerator.

You can be as creative with this exercise as you'd like. For instance, when you contemplate the loss of your caree, you can fill the box with photos of your caree, notes about what you miss most about your caree and what's hard now because your caree is gone.

When you think about losing yourself, you may fill the box up with a vision for who you want to be. Clip photos from magazines, articles from newspapers, notes you jot down, items you find during the day which strike you because they feel different or alien to you.

With this exercise, you lose the losses and keep the gains.

Memories

When you are the family caregiver you are the family historian. You have the memories. And, yet, you may worry that you will lose the memories.

During a lunch with Michelle Norman, who cared for her parents, I asked her what's difficult now, almost two years after the loss of her parents. As the tears flowed, she talked about the lessening of the memories. She struggles to keep the memories fresh. And, for her, her memories tie her children to her parents. Her children only will know their grandparents through Michelle's memories.

As you continue to preserve your memories of your caree, be sure to also record the details of your caree's life story. Your caree's life story affects your life story which impacts the future generations. Passing down the family history allows each generation to better understand itself. I spent time with my grandmother before she died so I could better know her. I later realized that understanding my grandmother meant I better understood my father which meant I gained greater insights into myself.

With the memories secured, you ensure your caree stays a part of the next generation.

Your Identify

Recently, I connected with Kristi Petersen Schoonover, a ghost story writer who, during her childhood, cared for her mother and then later, as an adult, for her father. Kristi joined me on my Internet talk show to share her story as a youth caregiver.

During our discussion, she said something really interesting. When she let go of her identity as her dead mother's daughter, her life got easier. And, in particular, Mother's Day transformed from a day of sadness into a good day.

The identities we take on during our life often seem to fit so easily. Until they become too tight and we literally can't function in them.

When you became a family caregiver, you took on the identity of caregiver. You took care, you gave care. You were the care. Others may have helped, including staff if your caree resided in a facility. But, when a decision had to be made, it was you.

The role of caregiver can become so intense that it becomes who you are. You become the one who is the first to do, to give, to care.

When a caree dies, you can feel like you've lost a job. Your role as a caregiver became more than just a job; it seemed to define you. And, then it was gone as quickly as your caree. Without that identity, you may wonder, who am I?

Interesting enough, what made you a family caregiver are the traits you brought to the job of caregiving. While it felt that caring for your caree made you a family caregiver, the truth is you had all the characteristics before caregiving that made you a caregiver. Maybe caregiving woke up those traits. Maybe caregiving honed those traits. But you had them before.

Which means you have them now.

So, although you may not be a family caregiver, you still have those traits that made you one. Your caree's death doesn't end who you are: Caring, loyal, committed, strong, persistent, resourceful, tenacious, smart, courageous, fun and funny.

You may lose the word "caregiver" but you never lose who you are. You've lost a job but you've added another dimension to your individualism. When Kristi opened up her idea of who she is, when she defined herself separate from her caree, she became content in her days, especially those days that had been difficult.

What you've gained in caregiving now becomes what's valuable as you discover yourself, your potential and your opportunities. Be open, now, to discover.

~ Discover ~

"The real voyage of discovery consists not in seeking new landscapes but in having new eyes."
~ Marcel Proust

During caregiving, you learned much about your caree, other family members and yourself. Chances are, you discovered that you can do what seems to be impossible.

In your life after caregiving, it's time to discover how to mesh who you are now with your new life.

During caregiving, you grew comfortable in taking care. It's what you did. It was who you were. Maybe you blogged about caregiving and enjoyed connections because of it. Perhaps you gained a following on social media because of your thoughts about caregiving and loved being known for that. Maybe you became a leader in your support group, a role you absolutely loved.

You can't help but wonder: Who am I if I'm not a family caregiver? As you moved forward, know that your ability to create what you loved in caregiving means you can find what you love after caregiving. You can blog about another topic, including life after caregiving. You can share your perspectives on social media, maybe now about what changes are needed in our health care system. You can continue to lead, maybe in your house of worship or a new group or club you join.

You also may feel a loneliness now. You'll also be alone with yourself. It may feel unsettling and scary to be alone. The aloneness is like an emptiness. You may be tempted to believe others can fill you—that friends, family members, work will add back to your life what you lost when caregiving ended.

The truth is that you are the replacement for caregiving. It's now your turn to be the watering can which nourishes who you are and who you can be. Depending on others to fill your emptiness creates an unhealthy expectation and dysfunction in your relationships. It's your life—it's your void. It's scary but it's also an opportunity. Take the opportunity rather than passing it on to another. This is your chance to be who you are, to step into your life. Discover what makes you feel good, rather than what you think will make others feel good about you. As you go through the discovery process, throw out any thoughts about whether or not others will like or approve of your choices. If you defer to others, then they live your life. Choose you—and that ensures others fit naturally, rather than forced, into your life.

During an interview for a podcast, Susan Smith, who cared for her mother, shared this coping mechanism when she felt the fear of the future: "I held my mother's hand all those years. I can hold my hand now."

You can fill your void by taking a closer look at what makes you. Let's discover your values, gifts, passions and purpose.

Your Values

What's important to you are your values. They are like your guiding light; when you follow your values, you end up home. When you dismiss your values by following another's, you end up locked out of their home. Embrace what's important to you because it's how you stay true to yourself. It's how you always stay home rather than knocking on someone else's door.

Your values led you through caregiving. Your value of responsibility, family, commitment and loyalty kept you in caregiving. These values will help now. Because you understand what you value, you can choose to spend your day in those values.

Your values can help drive your priorities. When you understand your values, you understand what's important, which means you make decisions about how to spend your day in a more meaningful way. If you value honesty, for instance, you won't waste your time in a friendship with someone who constantly stretches the truth.

You'll find a list of values on the next page. Choose three to five values that resonate with you, that describe your priorities.

List of Values

Accountability	Love, Romance
Calm, quietude, peace	Loyalty
Cleanliness, orderliness	Openness
Commitment	Patriotism
Communication	Peace, Non-violence
Community	Personal Growth
Competence	Pleasure
Concern for others	Preservation
Connection	Privacy
Creativity	Progress
Decisiveness	Prosperity
Delight of being, joy	Punctuality
Democracy	Quality of work
Discipline	Reliability
Discovery	Resourcefulness
Diversity	Respect for others
Equality	Responsiveness
Faith	Safety
Family	Security
Friendship	Self-reliance
Fun	Service (to others, society)
Good will	Simplicity
Goodness	Stability
Gratitude	Strength
Hard work	Succeed
Harmony	Teamwork
Honesty	Timeliness
Honor	Tolerance
Independence	Tradition
Individuality	Tranquility
Innovation	Trust
Integrity	Truth
Justice	Unity
Knowledge	Variety
Leadership	Wisdom

Source: The Power of Personal Values by Roy Posner

When you choose your values, write them down to use as reminders when you face decisions going forward. As you work to find the path to take going forward, your values light the way.

Embrace your values—they help you spend your time wisely.

Your Passions

While values drive your priorities, your passions fuel your life. Your passions make time pass without your notice. Your passions envelop your attention, they capture your soul.

So, what's your passion? It could be sports, it could WWII history, it could be a thought-provoking conversation, it could be fine wine. It could be adding to your bug collection, coding software, organizing activities in your community or running marathons.

It's what stokes the fire in your belly. And, it's just you. It's not about anyone else. It's what puts the zip in your step.

You may think that you've lost your passions to caregiving. Perhaps caregiving dulled your passions—now you're just looking to sharpen them. Think about what you enjoyed as a kid. What's a grown-up version of that?

You also can try this exercise to help you uncover your passions: You have a very small car, like a smart car. You can only bring what's truly important with you. What will you bring? If you think, I can't live without my pastels, then drawing with your pastels is your passion. If you can't bear to think about leaving your sewing machine, then sewing is your passion. If you can't imagine a day without your guitar, then playing your guitar is your passion.

You may also have a nagging idea in the back of your head about an activity or hobby you'd like to try. Write down those nagging thoughts.

Take note of your passions and then give those passions your time.

Your Gifts

We're each given gifts. The gift of acting, writing, painting, organizing, motivating, comforting.

What are you good at?

It can be difficult to see our gifts because our gifts are too close to us to see. So, call three family members or friends and ask: What do you think my gifts are?

As you hear about your gifts, consider: How can you give your gifts to the world? Giving to the world may mean giving to your home, your family, your community or truly the world.

Your Purpose

You may feel pressure to find a new purpose. Know that life is not about one purpose but many purposes. A purpose may be to be a dependable family member, a volunteer in your house of worship, a lover of good literature. Your purpose on some days may be to be a productive employee. And, some days, your purpose may be to simply make it to tomorrow. Know you can have as many purposes as you choose.

Your purpose doesn't have to change the world—it just has to give meaning to your world.

Your values, passions and gifts can combine into your purpose. For instance, you value giving back, you're passionate about your politics and you're gifted in organizing people. So, you could put all of that together to volunteer to run the local campaign for your favorite presidential candidate.

Or, you value integrity, you're passionate about teaching and you're gifted at mathematics. So, you tutor high schools kids in math.

When you add up your values, passions, gifts and purpose(s), you get you. You've found you. You may feel like it should be more complicated than this. Make it this simple. Don't overthink or overwork it. Once you figure it out, believe it. Don't second guess or doubt, don't wonder if you're being too prideful or egotistical. Instead, be grateful to be found. Now that you are found, you can discover how to be you in the world.

~ Experiment ~

"There's something liberating about not pretending. Dare to embarrass yourself. Risk."
~ Drew Barrymore

Four times in our life we hope for a miracle: As a family member lies dying, when we're out of money, when we're looking for love and when we need a job. We hope for a miracle that will save our caree, will bring in the money, will introduce us to our soul mate, will land us the job.

We so wish these miracles happen as easily as waking up one morning to find our caree alive, a pile of cash in the bank account, a job offer on the dining room table and our soul mate at the front door.

If only.

I believe miracles happen but only after we put in the hard work, after we keep going when really we would just rather give up. The overnight miracle comes after many hours of diligent work.

After caregiving ends, you may need a miracle or two. You may need to find a job yesterday. Or, you may decide this is the time to change careers. Or, you may decide this is the time to start a business.

As you can, experiment. Try out different options, see how they fit, understand whether they will work for you. Experimenting can be part of putting in the work. When you experiment, you may just find your miracle.

Any time you head out into the world to find a job or start dating or mull over starting a business, you will hear advice and opinions from others. "You were so great at caregiving—you should volunteer to help others." Or, "You should become a nurse."

Accept the compliments but defer on the advice. You may be completely burnt-out on helping and caring for others. That's okay. This is the time to nurture and care for your dream. How do you want to work for the rest of your life? What do you want to achieve? What legacy would you like to leave?

Most important, this is the time of life to figure out your why. Why do you want to start a business? Why do you want to switch careers? Why do you want to volunteer?

Your why will become your foundation from which all your decisions come. Your why most likely knows its source from one of your values. Because you value your family, you choose to take a job that allows you flexibility. Your why is your time with family. Why will you take that job? Because it affords you time with your family.

As you go through the process of experimenting, you can ask yourself: Why is this a good idea for me? Why do I want to try this? Why is this important to me? Understanding your why helps you feel good about your decisions. And, be open to the answer of "Why not?" In a time of discovery, why not?

As you go through the process of experimenting to find your next career or launch your business or re-enter the workforce, remember:

1. Experimenting means some of what you try will work and some won't. It's okay if an experiment doesn't work—it's actually why you're experimenting. You're looking for a fit and that means you have to try on different sizes, colors and styles. If if doesn't work, it just means it wasn't a good fit.

2. Experimenting means mixing and matching. It's all about thinking outside the box. It's about creating new rules, operating under different perspectives. If you want to try something that's never been done before, then go for it. Pave the trail.

3. Experimenting means you have no limits. You are just the right age, right now, to experiment. Let go of believing you're too old or too late. Right now, you're right.

4. Experimenting is about being curious. Consider your experiences with an open mind and throw away the judgmental thoughts.

5. Experimenting also means dumping the bad hand. If you try something and it doesn't work, dump it.

6. Experimenting is also about moving on with lessons learned. Dump what doesn't work but keep what you learned about why it didn't work. You're building during your experiments.

7. Experimenting really has only two requirements: A sense of adventure and a sense of humor. Be adventurous in your experiments because you don't know whether you'll have another chance to do what you can do today. An adventure can be as simple as signing up for a dating site or as complicated as planning a trip alone through Europe. An adventure can be having coffee alone in a coffee shop in a different town or asking a CEO you meet standing in line at the grocery store for a job. And, remember to laugh throughout. You've just been through the serious business of caregiving, which showed you the importance of humor. Enjoy the experiments with laughter.

Finally, an experiment isn't about finding out what you're not good at—it's about finding what's not good for you, which is how you find what's good for you.

Not sure what to try? Try this: You've just won $1 million in the lottery. How will you use the money? In which of your dreams will you invest? Suspend reality to understand what you want. And, remember, you have no limits. You only have opportunities.

During a period of discovery, you'll need inspiration. Some ways you can be inspired:

1. **Create vision boards for your ideas, dreams, experiments**. Your vision boards can be an empty journal that holds your ideas, or a poster board that features a collage of photos and words, or Pinterest boards that contain images you've found online. You can create a vision

board for each experiment, each idea, each dream, each goal. Perhaps you'd like to redecorate the house. You can create a board on Pinterest for the house redecoration project. Maybe you're hoping for a job in government; you can buy a poster board which contains photos of the politicians you respect and emulate.

2. **Read inspirational books and watch moving movies**. Stories of those who achieve and overcome will remind you that you can, too.

3. **Join a community group to connect with others with a similar goal**. Check with your local newspaper or on Meetup.com to find a group. If you can't find a community group, then join an online group. If you're hoping to write a book, then join a writer's group. If you hope to hit the speaker's circuit, then join a Toastmaster's group. If you want to lose weight, check out a local Weight Watchers group. When you see others achieve, you'll be encouraged to do the same.

4. **Watch sports, listen to great music, attend local theater**. When you watch others do well, you can catch their spirit.

5. **Staying inspired also means keeping the faith**. Find your favorite inspirational quotes and keep them nearby. Carry a small journal with your favorite quotes so you can easily refer to them.

6. **Take note of your success**. We tend to remember what didn't go well and overlook what did go well. In the journal that keeps your inspirational quotes, add the successes, both big and small. Your successes will build. And, it's easier to build on them when you remember them.

As you experiment, you'll encounter many firsts: the first day at a new job, the first time cold calling, the first time creating a resume, the first time sending a tweet, the first date in decades.

Facing a first can be intimidating, fearful, paralyzing. These tips can help you when you face a first:

1. On the first day of a new job or volunteer position or school, bring your lunch, snacks and a good book. If you eat alone at lunch, your book will keep you company.

2. Before you publish a first (like a blog post or tweet), sit on it for a bit, even overnight if that helps. Then, hit send. You can always delete if you change your mind.

3. Have a uniform—an outfit you rely on that fits comfortably and feels good--that you can wear on your first dates, interviews, day of a new job.

4. Write out your worries the day before the first. Then, create a plan to manage if a worry becomes a reality.

5. Begin as an observer—watch the interactions around you, the rituals which seem a part of the culture, the way business gets done. Smile and be friendly. Your first few weeks in a new environment is about learning the ropes and then forming friendships.

6. Make a practice run of your commute at the time you will be commuting before your first day. The practice run ensures you schedule enough time, become familiar with the unfamiliar and take the newness out of one part of your new day.

7. You'll have mishaps during your first few weeks. Acknowledge a mistake, ask for help fixing, then talk out a way to prevent.

8. Let family members know how they can reach you and that your priority during your first few weeks is your job. When you set expectations, you minimize some of the stress. If you are clear with family members and friends that they can reach you after work hours during your first two weeks at the new job, then you won't be upset and stressed if family members call at the worst time possible at work. You simply won't answer the phone.

9. Get ready the night before: iron your clothes, make your lunch, organize what you'll need.

10. When you get a tour of the office, take note of landmarks which will help you find the restroom, locate your department, get back to the elevator.

New can be stressful—it's also exciting. Work through your stress so you can enjoy what's in front of you.

Starting a Business

I've met many former family caregivers who have started a business to help current family caregivers. Some begin a home care agency, some start a website, some develop apps. Alan Levy founded blogtalkradio.com, which I use to broadcast my Internet talk shows, because of his experience blogging during his father's illness.

Look to others who have blazed the path before you if you're thinking about starting a business. Use the connections you created during caregiving—meet with the owner of the home care agency you used, the Executive Director of the adult day service, the administrator of the long-term care facility. You can ask them what it's like to run a business, what skills they feel are important, how you can learn more about starting and maintaining a small business.

As you think about starting a business, particularly a business for family caregivers, research what's already available in the marketplace. The business of caregiving is particularly difficult. You may have an idea for a service or product for family caregivers, believing that it's currently not available because you didn't know about it during your caregiving experience. I launched CareGiving.com in 1996—it's been in the same place for all those years. On a regular basis, former family caregivers will leave comments on the website wishing they had found the site during their caregiving experience. They can find it now but couldn't then even though it has never moved. It's the stress of caregiving. Just because you didn't know about it during your caregiving experience doesn't mean that product or service or technology doesn't already exist.

If you have an idea for a product or service for a family caregiver and discover it's already implemented and developed, then consider helping that company, either as a volunteer or employee. It's a product or service you believe in so you'll be ensuring its success in the marketplace. Reach out to the company, let them know you understand how important their product or service is to a family caregiver, that you would love to be a part of their team to bring the product or service to as many family caregivers as possible. Provide a brief background on your caregiving experience, explain what would have been different for you had you had the product and service. Then, ask: Who could you speak to about employment opportunities?

The stress of caregiving is also what makes it difficult to sell a product or service to family caregivers. As you know, the caregiving experience causes exhaustion, fatigue, anxiety, worry and short tempers. As a customer base, it can be difficult to reach and to serve family caregivers effectively. It takes patience and compassion to work with individuals who struggle with an intense stress. They will take their bad days and bad moments out on you. But when you help them, you will will be part of making their lives so much better.

Regardless of the kind of business you launch, starting and running a small business takes a huge commitment in money, time, patience and resilience. It will take you so much longer than you thought, you will need much more money than you expected, and it will require so much perseverance than you thought you had. I regularly watch *Shark Tank* on ABC, which shows you how to pitch your business idea to potential investors. I remember Robert Herjavec, one of the sharks, explaining that it takes 10 to 15 years to become an overnight success. It is hard work to start a business. It's also empowering and thrilling to have an idea that becomes a product or service that makes a difference for another.

Starting a business is a process, which can look like this:

1. **Research yourself**, suggests my dad, a counselor for Service Corp. of Retired Executives (SCORE). What do you enjoy? Would you like to run a part-time business, a seasonal business or a full-time business? What will work with your life today? Would you like to run a business on your own or find a partner? What do you know about yourself that will make your business a success? What kind of business will add enjoyment to your life? You must like your business in order for it to succeed.

2. **Research the marketplace**. Which companies currently offer something similar? What will differentiate your product or service? Why will a potential customer buy your product or service over the competitor's?

3. **Research the mechanics of running a business**. Talk out your idea with a counselor from SCORE or a staff member on the Small Business Administration, or take a class through your local community college. What do you do well? What can you hire out that you don't do well?

4. **Research how you'll get the capital to run the business**. Is it worthwhile to pursue investors? Would family and friends be interested in investing? Is running a crowdfunding campaign through a website like KickStarter an option? Could working another job give you the capital to start and maintain your business during its early years?

5. **Research how companies becomes successful**. *The New York Times* has great a column called "You're the Boss, The Art of Running a Small Business." I also regularly read Seth Godin's blog, which offers perspectives on how to do well in business. I don't always understand Seth's point but I always appreciate his push to make us best. Not second best. Best. Chris Brogan runs a blog called "Owner," which offers tips and insights on how to own well. Harvard Business Review's website often runs business case profiles, which help you understand the solutions to common problems.

6. **Research your marketplace and your customer**. Who is your customer? Why will your customer buy from you? Be sure to create a specific profile of your customer, which you refer to regularly.

For instance, my customer is a family caregiver. Often, others will mistake my customer for an older adult. An older adult could be a customer but only if he or she also cares for a family member or friend. I understand my customer which is why my content, products or services don't deviate from who my customer is. I've seen many other companies dilute their products and services by marketing them to seniors and to family caregivers. A senior has certain needs. A family caregiver has certain needs. If you try to serve both of those different needs, you run the risk of meeting the needs of neither. Understand your customer and keep the focus on that customer.

7. **Create a simple way to explain your business or product or service**. When it's simple to say, it's easy to sell. When it's a convoluted description, you'll find it difficult to find customers, much less sell to customers. Bottom line: What do you do that will be meaningful

to your customers?

8. **Before going to market with your product or service, research what the marketplace thinks of your product or service**. Organize informal focus groups of potential customers. Understanding your customer will be helpful now—you'll be able to concentrate your efforts on finding those individuals who meet your customer profile and asking them for input. Ask family members, friends, colleagues if they know of anyone who fits the customer profile to be part of a focus group. Then, ask for referrals from them to find others who fit your customer profile. Be open to criticism—it helps you improve your offerings.

9. **Launch your product or service, continuing to tweak it along the way**. If you wait until you have a perfect product or service, you'll wait forever. Change what isn't working as you go along and be quick to respond to customer feedback and requests.

10. **Create your support**. It's terrifying, nerve-wracking and exhilarating to go live. Have a team of support who helps you resolve problems, stay focused, overcome challenges. Your team could include a mentor, an accountant, a business coach, a good friend and a customer. You know what it's like to go it alone—make sure you get support and help now.

I regularly receive emails from individuals asking me to promote their service, feature their product on my website and plug their company on social media. Because I get so many requests, I wanted to offer some suggestions to help you when you approach others to publish your content, plug your work or review your product.

Some suggestions:

1. Get the name correct of the person you are contacting. I'm called "Diane," "Denis," "Debbie." You're already at a disadvantage when you get the name wrong.

2. Be sure you reference the correct business name or website. You may be sending out a message to several companies or websites. Double check that you've got the correct contact information for each one.

3. Be sure you understand the mission of the company you are contacting and that your request matches that mission. Because my site is about an experience (the experience of caring for a family member or friend with a chronic illness or debilitating illness or injury), it's best not to expect that I'll publish content specific to an age group. Again, we're about an experience, not an age.

4. I've received emails from those I don't know who want me to help them which include questions about my husband (I'm not married) and my children (I don't have any). If you are positive you know personal information about the individual you are contacting, then go ahead and mention it. Otherwise, don't and don't be tempted to guess.

5. Give people time to respond, understanding that your request often lands in an Inbox during a really busy day. And, send out a friendly follow up every few weeks. Don't take a lack of response personally.

6. Share how you think your work will fit with the work of the individual you are contacting.

Sell your work by illustrating how it will improve the individual's work—by bringing in money, increasing website traffic, add valuing to the current offerings. Highlight the benefits you bring to the table.

7. Timing is everything. I recently was harassed on Twitter and, because Twitter is public, the harassment was visible for my followers. About an hour after the interaction ended, someone contacted me to review her book, mentioning that watching the harassment gave her an idea of how I could help her. That was probably not the best time for her to reach out to me to ask me to do a favor for her.

8. Invest time in the work of the individual you are contacting. You are asking someone else to put energy into you. Do that first. Do your research, read the work, understand the mission. And, tell the individual what you like about his or her work.
9. When you follow up, include a reminder of why you are following up. We all receive so many requests for our time and help; it's difficult to remember all the requests.

10. Make it easy for an individual to say "Yes" to your request. Be brief, simple, straight-forward, kind and compelling.

Social media makes connecting so much easier—you don't have to try to find an email address or a phone number. You can just find the contact on Twitter or LinkedIn. One of the best way to raise your own profile is by promoting the work of those with whom you want to connect.

I love Twitter for this reason. I share (retweet) information shared by connections I want to make and who I value. You may be tempted to simply ask for what you want by sending a tweet ("Hey! Promote my book. Please RT!"). Every day, I receive tweets like this. I'm more likely to share about a product or service or company if someone representing the product or service or company has connected with me by retweeting my tweets, participating in Twitter chats I moderate and engaging me in interesting conversations. I understand everyone has an agenda. I find it works better if we put our agendas aside to first connect as people and then ask for help promoting a product or service or initiative.

Finally, whether you start a business or write a book, you'll need publicity. Subscribe to a free newsletter called Help a Reporter Out, which features queries for experts from reporters. When reporters need a source for a story, they'll use HARO to get the word out. It's a free service and it could garner some press for you.

Writing a Book

During caregiving, you probably thought, I need to write a book about this. And, certainly, caregiving has all the ingredients for a great book—it's a drama, comedy and mystery all rolled into one.

After caregiving ends, many write a book about their personal experience or a book of tips and suggestions to help other family caregivers. You may want to write a book about your caree's life story. You could write a book that focuses on your experience with the health care system, that features one life-changing year during caregiving, that illustrates how you and your spouse worked together to give your caree the best quality care. You could write a book about your caregiving experience but tell it through a series of short stories. You could publish a book of poems you wrote and include your photography. You can be as creative and innovative as you'd like.

If you want to write a book, you've got lots of resources available to self-publish. You could try to find a publisher but the quickest and easiest way to get published is to do it yourself. And, when you self-publish, you can sell your book through Amazon.com and other book sellers. When you self-publish, you only incur costs if you buy your books. You don't have to maintain an inventory of copies or commit to selling a certain number of books. You receive a cut of the revenue when a book sells. It's a wonderful and affordable option. (You'll find a list of companies that help you self publish in our Resources section.)

Before you begin your book, map out its organization. Consider: How does your story start? What parts of the story are most important to tell? Why do you want to share your story? How will you deal with the difficult and personal parts of the story? Would it be best to talk it out with family members and friends? How will you write about any disagreements that occurred with family members? Will family members give you permission to include these? If not, how will you tell a story without including the arguments? What do you want the reader to learn and know about your story? How do you want the reader to feel at the book's end?

For me, I find it overwhelming to tell a long story so I do better when I separate the story into sections. For instance, a caregiving story could be organized into the following sections:

1. Your caree lives alone and begins to need your help.
2. You begin to help and your family begins to fall apart.
3. You're helping more and trying to manage difficult family dynamics.
4. Your caree moves in with you; you and your family members call a truce.
5. Your caree dies in your home.

Once I've organized the sections, I tackle one section at a time. I won't perfect a section before moving to the next, though. I'm creating the framework for the book and then going back and filling in details. Because the art of writing is re-writing, I'll continue to revisit each section, adding more detail as I fine tune the writing.

Every writer needs a good editor. You can purchase editing services through a self-publishing company or hire an editor on your own or you can ask for help from a family member or friend. Check with your local community colleges and libraries about a writer's group you can join so you stay accountable to your writing. The group also may able be able to help with editing your work.

I've found that the cure for writer's block is to just simply write. Just write without worrying if the writing is good because you will rewrite anyway. Commit to the writing process by scheduling time each day to write, whether it be 30 minutes or two hours.

If you would like to write a book, you could start by creating your own blog through a site like wordpress.com or blogger.com. Tell your story through blog posts, then promote your blog through social media to build a readership. Strive to update your blog every few days—the fresh content keeps readers engaged and keeps you active on social media as you promote and share your content. When you've got readers, you've got potential buyers of your book. As you publish blog posts, save each post in a Word document which then becomes your book.

You also can contact caregiving websites and ask to submit a guest blog post about your story. Typically, when you contribute a guest post, you'll be able to include a link to your blog in a short bio about yourself included with the blog post.

Your book may not make *The New York Times* best-sellers list. The point really is to get your story out there, to create a tangible memory of an important time in your life.

Finally, the best way to become a good writer is to be a good reader. Read regularly to appreciate the art of writing.

Talking about Caregiving in Your Career

After caregiving ends, you may need to find a job. Or, you may decide it's time to change careers. Or you may want to look for a job which will support you as you start a business.

When you cared for a family member or friend, you were the CEO of your caregiving experience. It's an experience that honed communication techniques, challenged you to take on new responsibilities, that cut your problem-solving skills. And, as you look for a job, you can highlight your successes as CEO of your caregiving experience.

As you reflect on your caregiving experience, pull together the following information:

1. The annual budget you managed for your caree's care, including:
   - Medications
   - Rental equipment
   - Supplies
   - Help you hired
   - Services

2. The negotiations you held with companies and organizations which saved money and caught mistakes, including on:
   - Hospital bills
   - Insurance bills
   - Medical equipment bills
   - Prescription bills

3. Your advocacy which ensured your caree received the best care possible, including during:
   - Hospitalizations
   - Stays in a long-term care facility, including skilled nursing facilities and assisted living facilities
   - Doctor appointments
   - Meetings to discuss treatment options

4. Your management of personnel, including:
   - Home health aides
   - Companion sitters

5. Your systems you developed which helped you organize the following:
   - Medical paperwork
   - Medication schedules
   - Medical records
   - Receipts and invoices

After you compile your successes, you can add the caregiving experience to your resume. I've included examples of how that can look:

Example 1
Managed an annual care budget of $50,000 for my spouse, who suffered from COPD and arthritis. Negotiated 35% savings on her medical bills. Advocated for better care which resulted in my spouse re-gaining important skills, such as ambulation and speech.

Example 2
Oversaw a $75,000 care budget for my grandmother, who suffered from dementia. Hired and managed a staff of three who provided daily care. Acted as liaison between my grandmother's doctor and 15 family members. Regularly held family meetings to share updates, discuss the budget and answer questions.

Example 3
Oversaw a $20,000 budget for my mother, who had a stroke in 2004. Successfully advocated on her behalf to reduce the number of medications she took from 20 to 3, resulting in an noticeable increase in her quality of life.

Example 4
Managed a $55,000 budget for my daughter's care. Negotiated with medical suppliers to save 40% on the costs of her medical equipment. Found a $1,500 error on her hospital bill.

Example 5
Oversaw the care for my 92-year-old father, including his budget for care, his medications, doctor visits and medical records. Caught an error at the pharmacy in which the pharmacist dispensed the wrong medication. Created a system to organize medical records, lab work and medication schedules that was adopted by a 20-person support group.

The details on your resume about your caregiving experience can become the talking points you use during your interview. Be proud of what you accomplished during caregiving and use examples of what you did well—you organized, managed, negotiated, researched, hired, fired, communicated, resolved. Have a few examples of how you impacted your caree's life ready to use during an interview.

If you have an immediate need to find a job, contact temporary placement agencies, check with local home care agencies, take a few part-time jobs. You can offer your services as a companion for home-bound older adults or as a babysitter or as a pet sitter through websites like Care.com or SitterCity.com. You also can get paid to take on tasks and errands through a site like TaskRabbit.com. Look for freelance work through Elance.com and Guru.com. You may worry about starting a job beneath you. When you need money, no job is beneath you. I've worked as a cashier in a bowling alley, as a companion sitter for older adults, as a baby-sitter, in various retails positions and a few temp jobs.

When you re-enter the workforce, working temp jobs and part-time jobs can help you regain your confidence. You'll get re-acquainted with how the world works now. You'll make connections which can help you as you search for full-time work. You'll also cultivate references which will become critical as you become a candidate an organization considers hiring.

It's scary to go out there. You can, though. Have your resume with you and a ready "Yes." Go out on as many interviews as you can because it's all good practice. Maybe you don't get the job, but you may net a contact who can help. Most important, you'll get closer to the job you want.

Changing Careers

Perhaps you kept the same job during caregiving because you just couldn't stomach the idea of managing another change. Now that caregiving has ended you find yourself resenting your job, dragging yourself into work each morning. You're ready for different.

As you consider a career change, investigate options. Talk to others who have a career you'd like. Ask them for suggestions on skills, knowledge and experience you'll need. Follow those who have the career on Twitter—read articles they share, participate in discussions with them, ask them questions. Send a request to connect with them on LinkedIn.

Changing careers could also mean going back to school. You could continue to work your current job and go back to school part-time. Or, perhaps, you decide to leave your job and go back to school full-time. Choose the option which works in your life right now. School is not about an age but about a thirst for learning and growing. At any age, you can add to your education.

Finding a Job

As you look for a job or change careers, map out the process of finding a job. It's overwhelming to think of going from where you are now and landing a job. It feels like too much. Break out the job search into steps and tasks you manage daily.

Your process could look like this:

1. Attend one networking meeting for job hunters each week. (Check with your local social service agencies and houses of worship to find out about these meetings.)

2. Connect with three individuals each day on social media (Twitter, Facebook, LinkedIn) who work in jobs or industries of interest to you.

3. Spend an hour each day on job websites (like CareerBuilder.com or Monster.com) looking for positions for which to apply.

4. Spend an hour each day researching companies for which you'd like to work. Follow the company's management on Twitter, ask your network of family members and friends if they know anyone who works at those companies. Send requests to connect on LinkedIn to those who may be good connections for you. (I receive requests to connect on LinkedIn daily from those I don't know; they'll send a request as if we are friends. I appreciate receiving these requests and accept probably 99% of them. Send the request. If your request isn't accepted, simply move on. But, if it is, a door just nudged open a bit for you.)

5. Spend 30 minutes each day adding content (articles, resources, thoughts, ideas) to your social media accounts that represent your knowledge, expertise, interests. Not sure how to do this? Watch how others do it and then follow their lead. When I joined LinkedIn, I learned how to use the site by following the activity of one of my contacts.

Volunteering

As you look for a job, consider volunteering in the industry you would like to work in. Volunteering is a great way to get experience and create contacts which can help in your job search. Volunteering is also a great way to acquire skills you may need which you currently don't have. It's also a great way to continue to use the skills you'll want to use in your career.

You may feel pressure to volunteer to help family caregivers or carees. Remove the pressure from your shoulders. You may not be ready when caregiving is still so fresh in your mind and in your heart. You can volunteer where you want, doing what sounds and feels interesting to you. Maybe after a break from caregiving, you'll want to volunteer to help family caregivers. And, maybe not. Whatever feels right for you is right.

If you want to work at a company which doesn't currently have job openings, then call and ask about volunteering. You could check with Human Resources or with an individual in the department you'd like to work. If they are not able to take you on as a volunteer, then move on. If you don't call to ask, though, you'll never know.

Once you start volunteering and making connections, you can ask for suggestions on how you can secure full-time employment.

You also may choose to volunteer simply because you feel it's important. It's not about your career but about giving back. You could volunteer to help a cause that became meaningful to you through caregiving. For instance, Debbie Weiss, who cared her husband, Richard, organized a fundraiser through the American Cancer Society in honor of her husband. She formed a team called Richard's Posse to walk in a Relay for Life event in her community.

Again, give yourself permission to volunteer doing what interests you. You'll be a great volunteer when you choose an organization whose work and mission excites you. You'll be a begrudging volunteer if you choose to volunteer where you think you should but really would rather not.

Relationships

Most likely, your caregiving experienced changed you in a profound way. Your change means you may feel different in your relationships. You may have left some friendships in the past and now feel ready to form new ones.

You may have long-term relationships which feel out-of-sync to you. I had a friend who divorced her husband after her mother and grandmother died within months of each other. Their deaths made her look at life as a finite experience. With the time she had left, she decided she didn't want to stay in a loveless marriage. If you feel different in your marriage, consider a marriage counselor or help from other professionals like your priest or rabbi. Before deciding to end it, try ways to make the relationship better, to find a way to reconnect. Schedule regular date nights, make your marriage a priority, communicate your needs and wants. If you've done all you can to make it work and it doesn't, then look to end it.

You also can experiment with how you spend time in your relationships. You probably spent a lot of time inside during caregiving. How can you be out with your relationships? What activities would you like to try with friends, your spouse, other family members? Perhaps you'd like to try a new way to be with your friends—more open and assertive. Maybe you'd like to be more open-minded and less judgmental.

You also may be looking for new friendships, as the old ones no longer fit in your life today. Join activities in your community that you'll enjoy, which can be a great way to meet new people.

Put your energy into the relationships that energize you. Most important, be who you want to be in your relationships. If you were once impatient, be patient. If you were judgmental, be understanding. Learn how to be your best in your relationships with others.

Dating

Just like a job search, looking for a soul mate is a numbers game. You need to meet many people before you'll meet the right one. Which means you will putting yourself out there for the potential of rejection over and over.

Choose a vehicle through which to meet people—either online sites, social groups in your community, matchmaking services. Try all of them and see which works for you. Or, simply use the one you know makes you most comfortable.

Before you begin dating, take time to be clear about what you want in a life partner. You've taken time to understand your values. What do you value in another? Use the same list of values to understand what you want in a life partner. When you focus on the values you want, you'll choose wisely.

Whatever happens, don't take it personally. Remember that others you meet are looking for what you're looking for—love. Because you wish for love, you can wish them love. And, if they don't connect with you in their search for love, you can let them go with a wish they find their love. Rejection isn't about what you lack but about a lack of chemistry. And, chemistry is out of your control. It's there or it's not.

As you re-enter the dating world, you may worry about doing and saying the right thing. For instance, if you're worried about who pays, ask for feedback. Simply say, "I'm still new to all of this. What's a good way to work out who pays?" When in doubt, just ask. If the question comes out wrong, then say, "That came out wrong. What I meant to say is:..."

Tom, who came to my presentation hoping for dating tips, asked me lots of questions, including:

1. Women seem to show up to social events in pairs. How do I manage the pairs when I'm only interested in one?

2. How do I know she's interested?

3. How long do I wait until I ask her out?

My suggestion is to simply be a friend first because you can't know all the answers until you test the waters. When you keep the perspective of initially seeking friendships, you take the pressure off yourself and others which means you enjoy the connections more because you're at ease. So, simply approach all situations as a friend would. So, for Tom, he can talk to both women because he's approaching both as friends. If there's a spark between Tom and one of them, the spark will sort out the answers for him.

I think we try too hard and force too much. Enjoy the experience of meeting and connecting with others. Love will bloom when the time is right so trust the timing.

Be safe and smart about how you meet others for the first time. Meet for coffee at first, which has limited financial and time commitments. Be gracious if you decline an invitation to get together again. You can say, "I enjoyed meeting you. I'm not able to get together again."

Be open to possibilities and stay protective of your heart. Your love is worth winning. Give yourself time to find others with whom you have a connection and time for a connection to form.

Be kindly honest about your intentions, especially during a break-up. If you want to end a relationship, end it rather than dragging it out. You can say, "I can see we want different things so I think its best to part ways. It was wonderful getting to know you. I wish the best for you." Know that others can heal from any hurt they feel from a break-up. You don't have to worry or fret about their well-being. They can take care of themselves. You take care of yourself by remaining honest, gracious and open-minded.

You may wonder how much about your dating life to disclose to others in your life. If you've lost your spouse, your adult children may not understand your desire to date again, especially if they feel it seems too soon. In this situation, leave room for others and their emotions, which leaves you room to make the decision that's right for you. Acknowledge if others may be upset by saying, "I understand why you would feel uncomfortable about this. I loved your mother with all my heart. Which is why I want my heart to love again." You can listen to their concerns, consider their suggestions and then move forward with what's right for you.

Travel

We live in a big, wonderful world. It's a blessing to be able to explore it. You can think about traveling on day trips or weekend trips or week-long trips. If you are single, look into tour packages—know that many travel packages cater to single travelers.

Consider day trips in your car, where you hit the highway to head to a spot nearby for sight-seeing, lunch and wandering. Know these trips can be planned with others or simply done on your own. Research destinations, choosing spots that feature an attraction of interest to you, like a museum or historical event. Enjoy the planning process, which can be as fun as the trip itself.

If you're still getting your feet wet in your life after caregiving ends, then consider keeping your trips close to home. Take a staycation and enjoy the sights and sounds of your local community. Try a new restaurant, visit an attraction you've driven by but never visited, check out your local Visitor's Bureau for ideas.

You could plan a trip based on a theme, like visiting every baseball park in the country, or attending mass in historic Catholic churches or swimming in the best beaches on either of the coasts. You can try cruises, car trips, guided tours, bus trips, train trips, lazy trips to a beach, or busy vacations to a large city like New York or Chicago. You may want to plan a trip to see family members you haven't seen in years or take a trip to learn more about your family's heritage and culture. You can recreate a trip you took as a kid. You can organize a family reunion at DisneyWorld or a nearby campground. You can ask friends to join you for a girls' getaway spa weekend or ask the guys to join you for a fishing trip.

You can look into experience trips—such as living for a week like a cowboy on a dude ranch or working as a crew member on a sailboat. You can ride your bike across Ireland or walk along the Appalachian mountains. You can plan a trip based on restaurants featured on *Diners, Drive-Ins and Dives* on the Food Network television channel or follow the path of the Ingalls family through the Midwest as documented by Laura Ingalls Wilder in her *Little House* series of books.

If you're an older adult, consider programs through RoadScholar (formerly Elder Hostel), which mesh life-long learning and travel to create an experience of first-hand learning. You can travel alone or organize a group. You'll find programs throughout the United States and the world. You can travel on a budget and at the last minute. If you love to learn and travel, a trip through Road Scholar may be a great option for you.

You also can check with your local museums, senior centers or local universities or colleges (including your alma mater) about travel packages available. Once you start looking, you'll find lots of opportunities to travel.

Trips to Europe will amaze you—and make you want to visit as often as you can. My sister turned me on to travel guides from Rick Steves for trips overseas. I've found his suggestions and tour ideas fantastic and easy to follow. In essence, he does all the planning for you.

If traveling feels intimating to you, know you've traveled to a foreign land throughout your caregiving experience. Think about how you learned to talk medical speak, navigate the health care system, get the directions you needed to give your caree the best quality care. Caregiving turned you into a traveler. Now, you get to choose your destinations. Explore your world, going as far you want and for as long as you can.

Learning

As you head into the world and try, why not look into what you can learn. Take classes at your local community college, audit classes at your local university, sign up for classes at your local library. You can learn about gardening at a local botanic garden, about photography at a community college, about history at the historical society. You will find opportunities to learn online at sites like www.coursera.com. You can learn about online educational and cultural events at www.openculture.com.

You can taking acting classes, design classes, art history classes. And, it's great to take classes now—because it's not about the grade but about what you enjoy. Don't worry about whether or not you'll be good about what you're learning. It's only important that you look forward to it and have fun at it.

And, as you learn, consider ways you can teach. Check with your local community college or senior center about offering a class that you can teach. And, websites like Dabble.co provide opportunities to learn and to teach. If you're a master cake decorator, for instance, you can teach a class through Dabble.co. And, check Meetup.com to learn about local gatherings with others who share your hobbies and interests.

As you experiment, document your experiences in a journal, through photos, or on a blog. Your journey of experiments will become a new way you live life. You'll love keeping track of all your experiments, regardless of how you feel about the actual experiment.

~ Drive ~

"You've done it before and you can do it now. See the positive possibilities. Redirect the substantial energy of your frustration and turn it into positive, effective, unstoppable determination."
~ Ralph Marston

The experiments show you what you want. Experimenting got you out to try, to test the waters. Experimenting can be scary but it also can be fun.

When you take the wheel, you're in a commitment. You're changing careers, starting the business, taking that job, going out on dates. You're pursuing opportunities based on your values, your gifts, your purpose. You're stepping fully into what's next, putting your new plan out into the world.

Seth Godin often writes about being picked—that we hope we'll get picked, for instance, by Oprah or *The Today Show*. We hope our dream will come true when we get picked. Godin's point is that we have to pick ourselves. We have to make it happen. We have to say, "I'm the one to achieve this, to accomplish this, to make this." Picking ourselves means believing in ourselves enough to know that we can, that we will, that we are just the one to take on this mission, this dream, this goal.

Doing it—becoming the next you—takes courage. You're taking risks in your personal life and professional life. You're asking for what you want, which means you're putting yourself out there.

It's great to know where you're going. It can be hard to keep going. Let's keep you going.

Stocking Up for the Road Trip

When you pack up the car for a road trip, you decide on your route and your stops while bringing along supplies you'll need along the way. Apply the same kind of organization to driving toward your dream. You may set a budget and a time frame for making your dream. For instance, you may decide you'll start your own business and give yourself a certain amount of money and time to use toward growing it to profitability. If your business takes off within the budget and time line, great. If not, you'll make changes, which could include taking on a partner, scaling back to part-time or closing the business.

As you drive toward your dream, you'll need to take regular breaks. You understand what it's like when a part of your life, like caregiving, takes over all of your life. You can balance your dream with other parts of your life—your passions, your relationships, your down time, your travel. Live fully.

You'll also notice that other cars drive along with you. Connect and share with others pursuing their dreams. Share resources, ideas, tips and skills. The road has plenty of room; you don't have to compete for space. Be generous to others; that's how the road stays open to you.

Managing the Potholes

You'll do it. But living fully means encountering failures. Success is about managing those potholes you hit and understanding how to maneuver the car so it gets back on the road.

In his book, *The Dip*, Seth Godin talks about the heart it takes to keep going. Most people don't achieve simply because they give up when it gets hard. The thing is: It's supposed to be hard. And, here's where your caregiving experience will be so beneficial to you: Caregiving honed your tenacity, your patience, your strong will. You will need this now, as you set out into what's next. Because you will overcome, you will succeed.

As you date or work on your business or pursue your career, you'll have days that feel exhilarating. And, then you'll have weeks that feel like the pits. You may find yourself in a funk. A funk usually starts when fear hits. Be honest about what you fear. Is it the future? The changes? The rejection?

Maybe you feel like you've run into too many problems, too much rejection, too many challenges. You fear what you want will never happen. You fear that you're too old or too late. When you stay in a funk, the fear wins. Fear wins when you think: "Why bother? It doesn't matter." In essence, you're saying: "What I do doesn't matter. I don't matter." In a funk, you've lost.

The funk wastes your time. Your time is too valuable to waste. While it can't be avoided, the funk can be limited. Pull yourself out of it rather then dragging yourself farther into it. This is your time—use it wisely.

How do you free yourself from that funk? Some tips to help you:

1. **Let go of what you expected your life to be**. You may find yourself thinking, "Well, if I had family members who helped me, it wouldn't be this hard." Or, "Because I used up so much of my life as a caregiver, I'm screwed right now." Or, "I shouldn't have to be going through all this at my age." Let go of what you thought your life should be and focus on what it is.

2. **Know you're not "wrong."** You are right to go for what you want in life. It's good to go for it! Fear will try to keep you safe. You're ready for the risk because you just went through the best training program (caregiving) to prepare you for right now.

3. **Move**. Walk, work out. The activity will help lift your spirits and show you that you are in much better shape than you thought.

4. **Tackle one task you've been putting off**. Make the phone call about the job you want. Sign the paperwork to ink the deal. Send the email to pitch a reporter a story idea. Do it, then keep going. Don't worry about whether or not you receive a response, just keep going. The reward comes as you keep trying. If you don't receive replies, it's not a reason to stop. It's a reason to try another way.

5. **Delegate one task you hate**. Hire someone to write your resume, ask a friend to help set up your LinkedIn account, barter with a friend to help write your dating site profile in exchange

for helping to hire help for your friend's ailing parent.

6. **Change your day's schedule**. Maybe you're starting too late in the day. Maybe you're finishing too early. Look at your schedule and think about what you can change to help you feel better.

7. **Dream**. Visualize living the life you want. See it, feel it, hear it, smell it. Every day, give yourself time to dream. Living your dream in your mind helps you create your dream. And, it's also a great break from the setbacks and wrong turns.

8. **Tally what's working**, which means you make right now count. Don't count the number of rejections, the number of days you've been trying, the number of days since you've had a date. Right now is only what counts; tally what's going well in this moment. You're doing something right—put that success in front of you. We often focus on the failure which can stop us. Looking into our success fuels us. When you tally what's working, you can put your energy into making more of that happen.

9. **Stop doing what doesn't work**. I recently decided to stop taking situations and relationships personally. It's been one of the best decisions I've ever made. Whatever keeps you in a place of pain or in a party of pity, stop.

10. **Make a threat a possibility**. That neighbor who seems to always make the sale could intimidate you—which means he feels like a threat because you feel so inferior to him. He's actually a possibility. How can you learn from him? What could he share with you that could be helpful?

11. **Commit with courage to your choice**. Be proud of your choice. Don't explain or defend or discount it. It's yours—be proud of it. When you hesitate about your choice, you're sending out mixed signals, making it hard for solutions and resources to commit to you. When you embrace your choice, you'll be surprised at how much good luck you'll have along the way. Your decisiveness helped create the good luck.

12. **Live your life with gratitude**. Be thankful every day for a chance to live your life and for all the experiences your life gives you--the good, the bad and everything in between. Write down your gratitudes every day and particularly on those days when you feel discouraged and defeated.

13. **Get what you need**. Do your best to live like you live in a garden, surrounded by support and help. Stay away from the desert, which means you will be thirsty and longing.

14. **Fill in the blank: I love** _____. Remember who and what you love.

16. **You didn't get this far to quit**. It's difficult, it's overwhelming, it's scary. Keep going. Small steps each day take you to where you want to be.

In the moment, I've cursed a pothole that's caused a flat tire. As I replaced the tire, though, I usually found a better, more affordable version of the original. The potholes often force my hand—I must now resolve a problem, find a different solution. As you hit potholes, be open to learning and adjusting.

Be honest with your support system about the potholes you hit. Share what's happened so you can learn about options and hear ideas. Be curious about what caused the pothole, what can be different and better going forward. Use a pothole to your advantage, to improve and innovate. Your potholes can lead you to your competitive advantage.

Forming a Team for Your Front and Back Seats

If you went through caregiving alone, you understand how hard it is to be it everything—the Plan A, Plan B and Plan C. So, in this phase of your life, build a team. Have colleagues and family members who support and cheer you on.

When you go out and decide to be different, you'll face ongoing doubts and insecurities. "Am I nuts to think I can do this," you may think. You can do this and the biggest obstacle you'll face is yourself. Your fear will try to keep you safe—but safe isn't what you're going for now. You're working toward next and that's not safe. Next requires a step forward into the unknown.

Your team will become an important motivator for you to keep going. And, when you have a team in place who understands what you're going for—a different career, a new job, a small business—they can help you keep going.

You'll need a team member who shares your vision; this person will share the front seat with you. When you take your eyes off your road, this person will remind you of where you are going and why. Most important, the person who shares your vision will remind you of your why. For instance, this team member will remind you that you started your business because you found a solution that really helps. You can keep going because your solution deserves to be available to as many people as possible.

In the back seat, you'll want to gather teammates who:
    1. Make you laugh so you can cope with your stress;
    2. Make you think by asking you the tough questions you'd rather dodge;
    3. Simply love you because you need love on your journey.

These teammates can be members of your bereavement group, members of your family, friends, mentors, life coaches and pets. Some of the teammates may be volunteers, others may be professionals you hire.

You also can use vision boards to be your teammates. For instance, a vision board (either poster boards or Pinterest boards) that details your vision can be that teammate that shares the front seat with you. You can create vision boards that feature what makes you laugh, what makes you think and what you love.

As you recruit teammates, volunteer to be teammates for others during their drive toward who they are meant to be. Give and receive—it's the cycle that helps keep you in your best shape.

Sometimes, Flying Past the Flaggers. Sometimes, Slowing Down

When you set your sights on your achievement, you may find others in your life suddenly seem to sabotage your efforts. They seem to want to derail you with warnings that you'll never get what you want. They seem to want to pull you over and keep you in the back of the pack, where they feel most comfortable.

It's okay to fly past these flaggers, who talk from their place of fear rather than your place of confidence. When they try to take the wheel from you, simply say, "I've thought all of this through. This is what I want. I believe it's my chance to get what I want. So, I'm going for it."

If the flaggers seem determined to bring you down, you can limit the amount of time spent with them. Remember that you've created a team to bring with you to keep you on path—look to them.

You also may encounter flaggers who see danger or disaster in front of you. You'll want to slow down for these flaggers. For instance, going over budget would be a flag for which to slow down and investigate. Feedback from customers about a product that causes problems rather than provides solutions is a flag that needs your attention. Constructive criticism from a friend who works as recruiter when you're looking for a job is another flag to heed.

So, how do you know which flags to fly past and for which to take the foot off the gas? Understand the motivations behind the flaggers. Do they want you to succeed so they share information that will help you succeed? Or, do they want you to keep them company in the status quo? You're not working so hard to achieve the status quo. Take what will help you reach your success.

Handling Reviews

Whether you work in a Fortune 500 company, for yourself full-time or at the local retail store part-time, you'll be reviewed. You'll always hope for a positive review. The reality, though, is that you'll have reviews which, well, will leave you wishing you could crawl into a hole.

Graciousness is your best strategy, whether it be with your manager at work or a user on Amazon who reads your book. In the workplace, be open and appreciative of your review, looking at the feedback as a chance to improve, even if it's only a chance to improve how you handle being in the hot seat.

Reviews online can be a little trickier because you will be tempted to engage with a user who gives you a thumbs down or one-star rating. Take the feedback, consider if it could improve the product, and then move on without responding. Those who give you poor ratings are not your target audience. You want to engage with those who like your work, who believe in your work. Put your energy in them.

When you can, thank those who review you for the time they invested in the review.

Changing Course

You may have such a strong vision for your dream that you can't imagine not achieving it. Until a competitor with deep pockets opens a business just like yours. Or, a wonderful romantic relationship suddenly takes a nose dive. Or, your employer gets bought and you're unexpectedly downsized. Or, you decide that you've worked long enough for yourself and love the stability that working for a company affords you.

Changing course can be one of the best ways to stay on course. You'll be affected by situations and events outside your control. You keep control when you stay flexible about your course. Stay connected to your dream but not the path that leads to your dream. You can change course at any time—because it's your course to create.

Failure will be a part of your success. But, failure is not who you are. Your failures can't define you—only you can do that. You now understand your values, passions, gifts and purposes—these stay constant in your life. An ending doesn't end you. You continue because you have what's most important. A failure may trip you up, may cause you to take time to regroup. And, then you'll go to what's next for you. You always will continue.

In his book, *The Power of Intention*, Dr. Wayne Dyer writes about using a visualization to help manage your frustration and uncertainty when your goals seem elusive. When you don't seem to have what you want, he suggests hanging on for the ride, as if you are standing on a subway car holding on to a railing for support. Trust your ride, knowing that sometimes life has a better destination planned for you than you can ever imagine.

~ Share ~

"Share your knowledge. It is a way to achieve immortality." ~ Dalai Lama XIV

Because of your caregiving experience, you understand the meaning of life. You get what's important, the value of giving, the necessity of receiving. It's important you share this wisdom and life lessons with others.

You can share what you know in bigger ways, like writing a book or blogging. Or, you can start a support group for family caregivers in your community. Perhaps you volunteer to help a few family caregivers in your community. Or, maybe you are the go-to caregiving resource at your job.

As you share your wisdom with family caregivers, keep in mind:

1. Share about resources and solutions but **let go of controlling what family caregivers do with that information**. Let the family caregiver live their experience.

2. **Keep your story separate** from the family caregiver's story. Listen to their story without inserting your story because their story is not about your story. You can share your experiences and your solutions but be sure that they keep their story.

3. If you know of a resource or individual who can help, **ask for permission before involving that resource or individual**. When you simply insert yourself (or another person or a resource) without the family caregiver's permission, you are taking control and assuming you know best. Offer help—and then follow the family caregiver's lead. Respect that the family caregiver knows best.

4. **Support the family caregiver by listening and validating** their experiences.

Perhaps you share your lessons learned in an indirect way. Rather than connecting with family caregivers, perhaps you simply decide to live each day to its fullest. You choose healthy options. You say hello to strangers. You live bigger than you did before.

As a former family caregiver, one of the best lessons learned you can share is perspective. So many lose their perspectives during their days and then in their lives. They value possessions over relationships or power over teamwork. You can share the healthy perspective that you understand now because of caregiving. And, as you share, it's not about a lecture but about sharing a wise word. It's about calming the chaos and offering a hand. You know that life becomes about the moments shared—you can share this amazing piece of wisdom in how you interact with others, how you show up to gatherings and events, how you listen when others talk.

Your Life

I have a colleague I'll call Pat who experienced more pain in her life than anyone should. She's open about her pain, sharing publicly on social media when tough anniversaries arrive. I read her posts with interest and discomfort. I've often wondered what makes me at times uncomfortable with her public outing of her pain of events that happened many years ago.

It finally dawned on me: She's selfish about her pain. Her husband and children and other family members experienced the same losses. And, yet, when she writes, it's as if she alone experienced devastation. It's like she's missing an opportunity—the opportunity to share the pain, to acknowledge that pain is universal. Rather than doing good with her pain, she keeps her pain to herself. It's like she's the only one. She loses the chance to use her pain to comfort others in her life who share her pain. She's walled away, which also means she can't connect to others to heal her own pain.

As you go out into your life, you will carry your pain with you. Be unselfish about your pain; meaning, know that you are part of a world that houses people all experiencing pain. The awareness that pain is universal means you can listen when another feels pain, empathize when another shares about pain and connect to another in pain with comfort and care. You don't live alone with your pain, but live together with others in pain. It's not about you but about us and how we all move through pain in our life the best we can.

Karen Gurney, who cared for her brother and mother, said it best: "It was (and is) a blessing to be able to mourn with those who mourn and comfort those who stand in need of comfort."

As you take your life forward, you may wonder if you can. If you should. You may feel odd, unsettled going forward. Moving forward is not about forgetting or leaving behind. Just as you carry your pain with you, you carry your past with you. Because your past made you who are you today. You can only move successfully into your future when you accept your past, make the most of your present and make the best plans you can for your future.

Your life may become about travel or gardening or family. You also may decide you want to share your life by re-marrying or cultivating a close circle of friends with whom you spend a significant amount of time. The time to live your life is now. Caregiving may have seemed to take from you. Now, you can see that it gave you the tools, perspectives, skills and wisdom to continue into your life, to life fully each day.

As you live your life, live knowing a full life means both a life that contains joy and sadness, problems and solutions. A good life isn't a perfect life but about doing your best as you overcome challenges, embrace blessings and take your risks.
And, living a good life is not about waiting for the perfect moments to take a risk, to try something new, to take care of those important to you. You probably experienced waiting during caregiving—putting so much on hold until caregiving ended. You realize now that the solution is not to put life on hold but to move forward, even just a little bit, with what you want from life. You have this moment to make the most of your life. Don't put a moment on hold. Take it and do your best with it.

Your Dreams

Tom, who I wrote about in the beginning of the book, reminds us all that the road to getting what we want is believing we can get it. If Tom can go out at 79 and look for love, we all can go after our dream.

During caregiving, you probably heard all the time, "You have to take care of yourself to care for another."

This is very true. It is so important to take care of yourself, which means following your dreams. You are in the best position to follow your dreams when you are in your best shape, emotionally, physically, mentally, spiritually. When you care for your body, for your mind, for your spirit and for your emotions, you are poised to fulfill your dream. In the resource section of the book, you'll find a care plan you can use to stay well.

As you experimented, you may have realized you really were dreaming, trying out a vision for your life. Now, you have a clearer idea of your dream for your life. As you step into your dream, you may be tempted to dream another's dream—to make that dream, rather than your dream, more important. Or, you may hear from family members and friends who worry that you'll fail so try to protect you by keeping you from your dream. "It's too hard to do that," they may say. "You're too old to do that," they may reply. "You don't have the right experience to make that happen."

I started a small business to help family caregivers when no one understood what I was doing. I wrote a book to help family caregivers based on my experiences, rather than on research. I really followed my heart. I also really listened to what I knew to be true. People discouraged me from launching a website, which was my best decision ever. People tried to minimize what I knew to be true because I didn't have traditional research to back it up. And, yet, I still hear from family caregivers that my insights, without data from research to back them up, speak to them.

Remember that those nay-sayers are just noise to ignore. Listen to your heart, follow your passion, believe in what you can do.

Make your dream a reality. When you make your dream your reality, you become a dream-maker. You can show others how to do this. You become an example to all of us. You become the inspiration. When you live your dream, you make it possible for others to do the same.

As you think about your dream, know you can have as any many dreams you can dream up.

Consider:

- Where do you want to travel during your life?
- Who do you want to meet?
- How will you handle the next caregiving experience?
- What legacy will you leave to your family?
- How will you stay connected to who is important to you?
- How will you stay connected to what is important to you?

- How will manage the potholes you will encounter?
- How will you take care of what is important to you?
- How will you take care of who is important to you?
- Who will you turn to when you need help?
- How will you ensure the sun shines even during the darkest days?
- How will you live so you die without regrets?

You also live your dream when you live by your own personal code of conduct. In this book, we're looking at how to live with yourself. It's about how to be who are you meant to be. To uncover your personal code of conduct, consider these questions:

- How do you respond to life's challenges?
- How do you help others?
- How do others help you?
- How will others describe you at the end of your life?
- At the end of your life, for what do you want to be remembered?

When I think about living with myself, I think about these tenets for my own personal code of conduct:

- Choose brevity.
- Choose courage.
- Choose possibilities.
- Choose kindness.
- Choose forgiveness.

When I'm faced with how to manage a relationship or situation or experience, I can look to my own personal code of conduct to help me move forward. Now, it's your turn. How will you live the rest of your life?

Your dreams need your attention. You are ready, make them come to life. Go for it.

In Their Words: Life After Caregiving Ends

Former family caregivers tell us about their lives, from two months to fourteen years after caregiving ends. They offer their perspective in answer to these questions:

- What was the hardest time for you after caregiving ended?

- What helped you most? What advice would you offer to a family caregiver adjusting to life after caregiving ended?

- How would you describe your life today?

I asked former family caregivers to share their reflections in their words so you can see how each manages after caregiving ends. Each has their own story to share, as do you. As you read these reflections, take what resonates with you.

And, consider answering these questions every few weeks or every few months, whatever works for you. Your perspectives during your moments in time will show you how far you've come.

Two Weeks

The hard times are different at different times. There is no ONE hardest time. Immediately after he passed, it was hard just accepting that Richard was no longer here in the physical world. The house was empty. Getting into bed at night those first few nights knowing that I'd never again be able to hold his hand, or kiss his forehead, or run my fingers through his hair - those nights were hard. As the days pass, I'm learning to adjust to the empty bed and empty house, but I hate the finality!

For almost a year I felt like I was living in limbo--knowing deep down that he would never get better, but still praying for a different outcome and trying to be positive. Living for months not venturing far from the house, and only going for necessary trips (grocery shopping, picking up and delivering work, etc.) Looking forward to the time I'd be able to live without those restrictions, and feeling guilty for wanting to be free to live again. But now, two weeks later, I'm in a different kind of limbo. There are so many things that need to be done, but can't get done till I have death certificates. (They take forever). From the normal, like notifying the insurance company, to the little things, like canceling his cell phone service without having to pay an early termination fee. Even Facebook requires proof of death to "memorialize" a Facebook account.

I could say that the loneliness is hard. The boredom is hard. Both are true. But are they the hardest? No. I think right now, today, the hardest thing for me is the wait. Waiting for those death certificates so I can take care of things and move on. Tomorrow, missing him might be harder still.

What's helping me the most getting through the days (and nights) is staying busy. I'm a graphic artist/typesetter and I work from home and have for many years. I do several monthly publications, so there's rarely a time when there's not work for me to do. So when I can't sleep, or the house feels too lonely, I escape into work. When I'm busy I don't have as much down time to think and reflect and miss Richard. Is that healthy? Probably not. But work has always been my escape and it's how I get by most days. And, I've been planning a celebration of Richard's life. It's this coming Sunday. So I've been busy organizing that. I'm wondering how I'll feel when I won't have that, or anything new to keep me distracted.

The first couple of days I didn't think I'd ever stop crying, even though Richard's death was expected. And everyone said that it's okay to cry. The show of sympathy, the cards, the sentiments, the offers for help – all of those brought more tears. And each time someone shows compassion, fresh tears fall. Then there were days when I barely cried and I thought that I should be crying more – after all it was only a few days that he's gone. But what I've heard is true. There is no right way to get through a death of a husband (or a parent or a child or any other caree). And there is no wrong way. What worked yesterday to get through the day might not work tomorrow. You just have to learn to cope, and like the caregiving, this new roller coaster ride won't last forever.

Richard's been gone just two weeks. I'm still in limbo. I'm still on a roller coaster. I'm missing him terribly.

My daughter (and 17-month-old granddaughter) flew in three days after he passed. She said she believed I needed the distraction, the time to play with the baby. She said there would be so many people at the celebration that she wanted to come now, when I needed her, not when I'd be surrounded by so many friends and people wanting to pay their respects. Boy was she right! But as we were getting ready to head out to go to the park, I almost went in to tell Richard I'd only be gone an hour. Then I realized he wasn't here any more to tell and I didn't have to only be gone an hour. And the tears came. But those two days with daughter and granddaughter were EXACTLY what I needed!

I've started going out to dinner with friends--three times in the last two weeks. That's three times more than I've gone out to dinner in the last nine months. It feels good and it feels strange. And I hate coming home to an empty house.

So how would I describe my life right now? Day at a time, or maybe moment at a time. I'll be fine. I am fine. I'm strong… I sometimes just wish I didn't have to be.
--Debbie Weiss

Nineteen Days

After seven years of caregiving, the hardest part for me today is feeling displaced. Adrift in slow motion with no direction.

What helps me the most is my faith in Christ. I hold fast to the truth that He will never leave me. He has a plan for me. I just have to be willing to wait for it and accept it.

Honestly I don't know yet what advice I feel I can offer anyone other than just get through the moments. You can't avoid them, eventually they will catch up to you, so just face them no matter how hard they are and get through them, one at a time. It's okay to cry. It's also okay to laugh.

Today my life feels uncertain and in slow motion. Uncertain because we never planned for our future. Many decisions will need to be made. Decisions I can't think about today, no matter how hard I try.

So many changes to make and things to do. Overwhelming to the point of tears sometimes over the simplest things, like adjusting the grocery list to exclude the items my husband only liked.

I have "mush brain." I can do things that are trivial and don't require much thought. The things that I have to exert brain energy for become an emotionally and physically exhausting chore. Even this simple questionnaire has taken me a few hours to answer.

I do know one thing, though. I will be okay, no matter what. I will be okay.

At age 51, I start a new chapter in my life. My 76-year-old husband of 32 years was diagnosed with Lewy Body dementia in October of 2007. On February 11, 2014, my full-time caregiving for him ended.

I may not see God's plan for me completely but I trust Him with my life and my heart.
--Kathy Lowrey

Two Months

(The hardest part) for me it was the sudden loss. I had just gone to see my mother the night before, she was doing great. About four hours later, I woke up with the call that she had been taken to the ER. I remember walking down the hall of the skilled nursing facility four hours earlier, thanking God for healing her and thinking life would be back to normal soon. She would be home in October (this was July 31st). I was walking on a cloud, life was great. Then four hours later, it was all over. She was gone, I now had to rebuild my life.

I also started to understand there was a cost to my caregiving. I did not see it at the time, but I had built my life around my mother. It's something that had to be done, my mother needed that. But, there was a great cost to me. I was out of work for seven years, my life revolved around my mother. I was happy with that. I would do it all again, if given a choice. Being her caregiver was the greatest job I ever had.

I was also blindsided by the reactions of some of my family. When I was in the ER after being told my mother was on life support, I called one of my siblings at around 2 a.m. I told them what was happening, that Mom's heart had stopped but they had gotten it started again. Their first words to me were, "Don't tell anyone, don't talk to anyone, don't call anyone and, for God sake's, don't post it on Facebook." I was stunned and angry. I did not show it at the time. I held my peace. The first thing I did when I got home was to leave my younger brother a message, go on Facebook and post to the family what had happened to our mother. They also tried to stop me from showing any grief on Facebook. I finally cut them off. Other things happened with other members of my family. My message on this is to be aware that some family members may blindside you with their reactions. Sometimes you have to cut them off and ignore them.

I had a talk with a friend shortly after my mother passed away. He put things in perspective. He said, "John, you are paying the price for caring. You built your life around your mother; there was nothing wrong with that. You did the right thing, but it comes at a cost." It helped me to understand the real reason I was grieving so much.

Seek out sites like where other caregivers will understand. Most people will not understand your grief, only another caregiver will. Cut off people who tell you to get over it or try and tell you they feel the same grief. Unless they've been a caregiver, they really don't understand.

Rebuilding my life has been slow. My mother has been gone two months and I'm finally out looking for work. In the next few weeks, I'll look at churches in the area to get my social life started again.
My older brother moved in with me days after our mother passed away. The first month was very hard. I was grieving and then having to adjust to another person in the house. Right now, it's going very well. I'm actually helping him find work and make a resume. (He hates computers so I help him.)
--John Barry

Three Months

The hardest part about my dad's death is not being able to talk to him, seek his advice and share things with him. My mom has dementia so my dad was the person I usually talked to about important things. He was a very logical, practical person and was able to guide me in making decisions. He was a very intelligent, well-read man and I loved sharing interesting books, movies, articles, and experiences with him. He shared in my love of intellectual pursuits and loved to discuss these things. There is no one in the world like him. I miss him terribly

My dad also helped me cope with my mom's dementia. He was a big help to me in that area. Now I deal with her by myself.

It's been very hard for me to understand how a person can just be here on this earth one minute and gone the next. When I look back on my dad's intelligence and accomplishments, it's hard to understand how all that can just be gone. I hope he was able to carry all of those things with him to an afterlife.

It helps me to be around friends, family and loved ones. I have also been reading a lot about near-death experiences because it helps to give me faith that there is an afterlife and that I will be reunited with my dad again. I want to believe that my dad is happy and at peace.

Sometimes the role of caregiver becomes our identity and we don't know who we are anymore when we no longer have that identity. You need to find your new identity once the "caregiver" identity is gone. This is the time for them to now take care of themselves and carve out a life. It is a time to pursue all those things they've always dreamed about, but were never able to do. Build a life they'd like to have. Focus on friends and family. Find something that fulfills them – be that spending time with friends, family or doing volunteer work. In their volunteer work, they may find people who need them just as much as the person they cared for needed them.

I now spend time taking care of my mom who has dementia. I am trying to stay in touch with family and friends. I am also trying to pursue things I'm interested in so that when my mom is no longer here, I won't be totally lost. I do worry about what my life will be like when she is gone since I am still in the caregiver role with her.
--Kelly Loeffler

Four Months

On the day my sister died, I felt grief mixed with guilt. Guilt that I could not do more for her and that I was relieved she was gone. Now, I mostly deal with guilt and an overall feeling of emptiness. I am consistently surprised that I forget she died and will often answer the question "do you have any brothers or sisters?" wrong. I look at her life and I am struck by how easy it is to slip into oblivion. I worry that I, too, will disappear when I die. I want to feel her loss more deeply. I miss grieving for her and I wish I could ask her, "Did I do enough for you when you were alive?" or "Do you forgive me for not doing more?" The realization that I will not get an answer is perhaps the hardest thing for me to accept. I have found that when I am honest about my often-conflicting feelings—sadness versus relief, emptiness versus remembrance and understanding versus bewilderment—do I find some sort of peace.

Be honest and be aware that there is nothing linear about your recovery from your loss. Some days will be better than others and some days worse. Some days your memories will be warm and on others they will not. There will be days when you are glad that your loved one is gone. Maybe it is because you are glad that they are out of pain, but it may also be that you are glad that the terrible burden has been lifted off your shoulders. Become comfortable with simultaneous truths. Denying them will only tie you up in emotional knots.

Life truly does go on. I get up and go to work and do the things that give me pleasure and try to minimize the things that cause me pain. I often talk to my sister in the same way we talked when she was alive. Sometimes that gives me comfort, sometimes it saddens me. I wish that one day I will come to some sort of understanding, but I know I won't. Peace is the best I can hope for and some days I have it.
--David Taback

Eight Months

The hardest time for me was the guilt. Looking back, the "should haves" and "could haves" even though I know going back wouldn't have helped Mom's disease. This, mixed with the feeling of relief when it was over. That has to be the worst. I'm relieved she is no longer suffering but wish she was still here and things were different. The heart-wrenching pain of thinking back at the moments that Mom didn't recognize me anymore. I still have moments of anxiety, fear and anger. The sorrow of still processing that Mom is no longer with us and that one day I won't remember the sound of her voice and what she was like before Alzheimer's struck her down. Sometimes I feel lost. She was my focus for so many years that I need to "re-learn" how to live without that role.

Being a caregiver to someone with Alzheimer's can be very isolating. People are afraid of it, don't understand it and, for the most part, don't understand why you would ever want to be such a caregiver. So in my case, I lost many of my "friends" and my social life virtually became non-existent.

I wouldn't change a day of it and, if I had it to do again, I would without question. I know Mom would have been proud of me for doing so.

That guilt is a natural reaction and so is relief. But, please, don't torment yourself over this. You were there for your loved one when it mattered the most. The relief, I believe, stems from the fact that your loved one is no longer suffering and the guilt, well, we're human. The grief will come and go. Let it happen as it may. If you need to cry, then cry. It relieves the stress. If you feel anger, let yourself be angry. It's a mix of emotions for you--the why's and what-if's. Find a way to relieve that anger--go to a gym and find a good punching bag or to a trusted friend or family member you can talk to or to a support group of people who have been through the same and understand. Hearing your situation through others really helps you to believe that you did everything you could and that you did it all right! Don't go through this alone. Talk about the happy times--don't just remember the Alzheimer's.

You have to remember that grief for Alzheimer's caregivers is unique. It doesn't subside as with other illnesses and diseases. Witnessing your loved ones loss of control of their physical and cognitive functions is heart-breaking. I have come to know it as "the long good-bye." It will come and go. It will lessen at times and magnify at times but please, always, always remember that if your loved one could have told you, they most certainly would have told you how very thankful and proud they are for and of you.

I am proud to have been able to take care of Mom until the day she died. Not having to put her in a home was very rewarding. I went in to this "caregiving" role completely unaware of what it meant--the depths AND the rewards. It has shown me a new part of myself - that anything is possible and that you have this unknown strength and uncanny ability to do what needs to be done. It has expanded my heart. It has shown me understanding that I never had before, patience that I never had time for and the sheer knowledge that it is really true when it is said to "not sweat the small stuff" and "stop and smell the roses." How quickly your life can be cut short and taken from you for any reason. I am much more aware of my surroundings and what is truly important. I have changed the markers by which I lead my life.
--Ericka Simon

I think the first three to four months were the hardest, the fact that I did not have anyone to come home to and care for. And the fact that after my wife died the calls of concern got less and less. The visits from friends and family got less and less. And very few wanted to talk about my wife, they were afraid they would upset me. So the first four months were the worst because I thought something was wrong with me.

I don't know if you believe in divine intervention, but I was lead to a pamphlet that had been in my wife's Bible for years. I read it and it changed everything. The title of the pamphlet is "When a Friend Experiences Tragedy, To Help You Help Those Who Mourn." After I found it, I wrote a letter to my friends and family and sent it with a copy of the pamphlet.

The pamphlet said, Don't tell people that "God will not put on you more than you can bear." It's ironic that today a very close friend gave me an article about this. Come to find out, God does not say this in the bible and I can't tell you how many times friends and family have told me this.

Finding and reading the pamphlet and understanding that most people don't know how to comfort the mourning has been most helpful to me. What we need is just a friend to tell us they love us, give us a hug and check on us and sit and listen and hold our hand.

My advice would be to continue to trust in God no matter how hard it is or how hard things get. Don't be ashamed of crying. It's been eight months since my wife died and I still cry every day. I have good days and I have bad days. The pain of the loss will not go away; it will just become less severe as time passes.

How is my life today? I still lonely but I'm trying to meet and make new friends. I'd like to start enjoying life again. But we who have lost lifelong mates must be very cautious because we are so tenderhearted. I don't know if I will ever re-marry, that thought is hard to comprehend. It takes a lot of time to sort things out and find your way in life. I still haven't found mine yet.

I guess the reason I'm sending this is because I was looking for some more insight from others who have shared the same experience. I read a post last night about how others deal with anniversaries and holidays. And I read where one lady just had a quiet day without guests and friends so she could reflect on the memories. I could relate to that because I did the same thing on our anniversary recently. It was just me and all the memories and pictures and cards. Several people couldn't understand that I just wanted to be alone and go back down memory lane. It was something I had to do.

I spent Christmas at our lake house with our dog. I couldn't be around all the merry stuff this year.
--Tom Boyd

(Editor's Note: Check with your local hospice organization about a pamphlet you can send to family members and friends to help them understand your grief.)

Nine Months

The fact that, regardless of what I am being told, it is not getting any easier to accept her passing and the realization that it may never be possible. We had been with each other almost every day of our lives, from the moment we first met as teenagers over 60 years ago. Hardly a day goes by without encountering something that reminds me of her.

During all those years that I cared for her, I could not bear to think about her leaving me, and how I would ever cope with the immediate aftermath...her wake, her funeral and her burial. I never thought beyond that point.

I am very blessed to have a supportive, loving family and a number of close friends who I see as often as possible. I also have a wide variety of interests, writing, reading, traveling and a number of physical activities which I pursue. Fortunately, I enjoy excellent health, and am able to bike, kayak, sail and ski on a regular basis.

My faith in the belief that we will be together again...some day....some place....sustains me through the darker moments.

Each of us has to find his or her own way of filling in the chasm that was once, I believe, part of our life's purpose, caring for someone we loved. Nothing, of course, will bring them back, and you have to fill in that void as much as possible by leading a full life, whatever that might be. For me, it is family, friends and intellectual and physical pursuits and faith. You must find your own way.
--Robert Semenza

12 Months

When you are a caregiver, whether it is for a spouse, parent, family member or friend, you always know that there will be an end that also means your loved one will pass away. I was involved for years with the slow decline but didn't know what it would be like for me once on the other side. I was a caregiver, a "stay-at-home daughter" and would cling to my mother's every breath.

Then the end comes, the grief fills you and the emptiness is overwhelming. Reliving the hard days, the sleepless nights and knowing that most people would never understand what my family and I had been through was extremely difficult. The void is so huge and now what? For me the hardest part was having all this knowledge and life experience that we lived through and not knowing where to place it. My decision to volunteer and then work for the Alzheimer's Association was probably the best undertaking as it allowed me to heal, help others and join with those who were like me. They got it and I was not alone as I began my new journey.

I gave myself time to heal. I didn't rush it. I allowed myself to realize it took many years of me dwelling in this dark place and therefore it will take some time to move forward. Grief is different for everyone so accept when the emotions come.

Surround yourself with great reminders of your loved one's past life. Who they were before and share those happy memories. Allow yourself to let good times and stories replace those days of caregiving and defining that person only as someone with the disease. Celebrate them and know that the privilege of caregiving is just that. You were someone's advocate, their physical, emotional and spiritual support as their life's last chapter was ending.

I never expected to find true joy fully again and then my life slowly moved forward. I take my loved one's memory along with me. As with most people who deal with this disease, I really thought the caregiving mindset would remain. Then living itself healed me and I am whole. For me, I think only of the good times we shared, lend advice and support to others, and embrace each day with a positive zest for the life I have. I would never trade those long, lonely, sad days as they shaped me more than any other period in my life. All I am I owe to my mother.
--Susan Smith

My caregiving was different in a sense than most. My husband was a brittle diabetic for 43 of our 49 years of marriage. He eventually lost a leg and his vision but remained busy until almost the end. For most of those years, I was on him constantly not to think of his diabetes as a liability, to encourage him not to think of it as a disability. We also made a lifestyle change when we sold our home and moved to Northern Wisconsin to open a Bed & Breakfast. That was a new career for both of us and we ran it as partners. We each had our own job and my shy husband became more outgoing. We were both involved in our small community

My life today, one year later, is changing drastically. I've sold our home and closed the B & B. I'm moving into an apartment (on the second floor so I can continue to use stairs as an exercise!!) and continuing to be involved in the community. I also have some travel planned for the next year.

My best advice is to be involved in your community and make many friends. I don't have much family here. My daughter and two granddaughters (22 and 18 years old) are here, my son and his family are five hours away, and my only brother lives in Canada. My support system comes from the many friends and co-volunteers and repeat B & B guests who stay constantly in touch. The family support is wonderful, but friendship is unconditional. I think (and my friends agree) that I've made a very good adjustment. I don't dwell on what could have been but instead on what my future holds.
--Bess Aho

Fifteen Months

I have challenges and successes being an aftergiver. I have learned that I am only happy if I choose to be. Hubby's passing will always make me sad, kinda like having a permanent flu. But instead of allowing that to depress me, I have the power to shift that and use it for a greater good.

If you have ever lost power for 24 hours, it's like that except that the power controls your water, heat, ability to breathe and everything else in life. I heard once, "It's like losing your right arm permanently."

Before his death, we had lots of discussions about what we were scared of, what we wanted for each other, what we wanted to make sure was taken care of and that we would always love each other, no matter what.

After his death, talking with friends and family and mostly my young daughter helped.

My faith and my belief in myself also help. I learned how to be a single mom which is very scary especially when you no longer have Daddy to back you up on discipline or when you want to share accomplishments.

I am grateful for my faith's traditional one-year religious observance of the mourning process. It has given me time to adjust and address many concerns involving my husband and how my daughter and I relate to his death and to each other.

I am also grateful that I was gifted with the honor of being a part of his life. The eternal blessing is our daughter who will always be the best of both of us. I will live knowing that he taught me so much about life, that I am strong, brave and have a tendency to be passionate about issues that will help society.
--Laura George

Sixteen Months

I think that the hardest time for me after caregiving was after my father's memorial service. I had devoted all my thoughts and time to him for three years. Even if I was not physically taking care of him, I was worrying or "on call" for the next crisis.

As life returned to normal and my children were back in school and family had left to go on with their lives, I was left not knowing what to do. I had to figure out what to do not only minute by minute but on a bigger scale. I had put my whole life on hold for my father. The experience had changed me in so many ways. Very little of what I had been doing before he had became ill seemed like anything I wanted to ever do again. The process of changing roles between my father and I (he became my baby and I the decision maker) had completely changed me. It had, in a way, freed me.

I had become an adult. My father had been a very domineering and controlling father, a very successful and eccentric man. It had seemed like I was always in his shadow, always a little girl. Now, I had grown up. I had become me. The things that I had faced emotionally, spiritually and physically had shocked every part of my being. The visions still shook me and overtook me with frequency. I had no idea how to do anything but meet the needs of my other important role – being a mom.

I realized I had always been a caregiver. My teenage years were spent as a co-caregiver with my mother for my paralyzed grandmother who lived at home until her death. Most of my years as an adult had been spent in inappropriate relationships where I tried to care for the wrong men and make them "better." I decided it was time to accept my caregiving personality and apply it both to those in need and in a manner where I would gain financial stability for my family. At 48, I decided to re-enroll in school to earn my nursing degree. I also took up fencing as a sport. In the short run, fencing helped me focus and gave me something to do outside of missing my dad.

I am a writer by passion. But for the first time, I would sit and try to write about my experience and the pain would overtake me. I process my life through writing but this time I could do nothing more than write a few lines and then I had to stop. I decided to just have an open page where I would just write the few sentences that came to mind and later, when I could, I would revisit those feelings and write about them.

Enrolling in school was the best thing I did for myself. I took both classes for my nursing degree as well as classes to become a EMT. I joined an ambulance core and could spend some time caring for people in a positive way. I am still in school and will complete my degree in the next two years.
Today, I am able to write about my experience caring for my father. It is what seems to be an unending revelation of what that period meant to my life. While I miss my father terribly, the intense visions have melted away into memories. My acute pain of missing him has dulled to an emptiness I will never fill. There are moments when I wish I was still caring for him. I have had some life-changing revelations about our relationship. As sad and completely overwhelming as the years where, I did not comprehend their significance as I was going through them. In addition to being a mom to three children and going to school full time, I have filled the empty spaces in my life by hiking, writing and reading as much as I can.

The period right after caregiving ends is a time of intense emotions, grief, visions and confusion. The swells of grief and intense emotions and emptiness will still come, whether you are busy or not. I feel it is very important to allow the process of time to heal.
--Victoria Sanjuan

22 Months

The hardest time for me after caring for my mother ended involved my father and I navigating our new relationship. At times, it seemed like the common goal of helping my mother and advocating for her was what held my relationship with my father closer. After my mother's death, I think I was a big reminder of that painful period in his life and he wasn't available for me emotionally and not as connected to me emotionally as he once was. It was really hard for me to deal with and felt like a betrayal. It's been a struggle.

What helped me most was seeing the end of caregiving as an opportunity for me to strike out on my own and start my law practice. This helped me to get through the rough patches of grief and see the positive in the struggles taking care of my mother. I also attended a grief group a few months after my mother's passing which was really helpful. I waited until I had a little perspective and did not go right away; I think that was best for me.

My advice for a caregiver after caregiving has ended is not to beat themselves up about any things they did or didn't do when they were caregiving for a loved one. They should be kind to themselves and allow themselves to grieve the experience. Caregivers might not have perspective right away on how this experience shaped them or the meanings of "why" they had to go through this experience. I believe that everything happens for a reason and try to appreciate the strength the experience gave me.

My life today is great and I believe a bit part of that is my attitude toward the experience. I appreciate the strength it gave me, I am proud of myself for taking the lead and having such a powerful role in the life of someone I deeply cared about. I have used this energy to start a business and survive the economic struggles that come along with caregiving.
--Kate Curler

Two Years

As background: I cared for my mother for several years prior to her losing her right leg at age 86. My caregiving experience then became truly intense. I was still the primary breadwinner for our household. My oldest brother also lived with us and stayed with Mom during the day while I was working.

At the end of May 2010, my brother had a stroke. I then had two people with very different needs to care for. Thanks to my brother's friend, who came in during the day, I was able to continue to work. This was a very grueling period for me.

My brother died on December 10th, 2010. After my brother died, I still had my mother to take care of and my job. I prepared to retire, hoping to devote my time more fully to taking care of my mother.

Four months later, on April 19th, 2011 my mother passed away. Even though we all understand that death will come to those we care for, and even though we may expect it, it still comes as a shock. Caregiving and loss go hand in hand. When caregiving ends, it ends with the death of one whom we love. Everyone's experience of caregiving and of loss is different and yet similar.

During the time that I cared for my family members, I came to know them so much better than I ever would have otherwise. We shared some of life's most difficult moments. They also shared so many of their thoughts and experiences with me that I would not otherwise have known. Likewise, I shared my daily experiences with them. I learned to love them more deeply during this period.

I found that my caregiving experience was intense and continually became more so. As I learned to deal with current challenges, more popped up. And then, suddenly it was over. Caring for my loved ones had become the focus and purpose of my life. Now what?

It took me a long time to figure out the "Now what."

A person whom I admire recently said to me, I believe that we are here for three reasons: one, to love others; two to learn and grow; and, three, to serve others. This echoes what I have always believed. However, I would probably combine two of these. I believe that when we love others, we want to serve them and when we serve others, we learn to love them. And I believe that all of these experiences help us to learn and grow to be better people.

During most of the first year after my mother died, I was in a very dark place. I really found it difficult to get out of bed, to get through the day, and to deal with the quiet. Many times, I went out to eat, to have a manicure, to a movie simply to get out of the house. I visited family. I had friends who dragged me out. Did any of it make me feel better? Not really, but it did get me out of myself for a while. I also, unfortunately, spent money that I should not have on things that I thought would make me happier.

And then I was asked to fill a service calling in my church. In order to do this, I had to get to know more about the people than I had before. I once again realized that each of us has our own story, our own problems, our own pain. I have also come to realize that my own experiences have put me in a position to be more empathetic. I can connect with many people because I, too, have suffered. I have also learned that there are many people who simply take advantage of everyone whenever they can. My hardest lessons recently have been to avoid being a patsy and to know that I deserve respect.

During my caregiving years, my mother became such a great example to me. She got up early every day to study the scriptures. She read every day, throughout the day, for both knowledge and entertainment. She found some way to help others every day; when she became physically incapacitated, she made it a point to call family and friends to listen to them. She spent time every day in trying to take care of her physical health. She walked for as long as she could and did the strengthening exercise the doctors gave her.

I am emulating my mother. I am trying to make it a point to learn something every day, to devote part of the day to spiritual growth, to spend some time each day taking care of myself, and to find ways to be of service to others each day. I try to remember that because you can't give away what you don't have, I need to strive for peace, serenity and love in my own life. And I now enjoy the quiet because it is no longer the reminder of those gone, but a sanctuary providing time and space for renewal.

If I had to give someone advice in the face of loss of a loved one, I would say:
- Give it time. Try to remember that time heals.
- Get up, get out of the house, and do some simple enjoyable things for yourself.
- Don't make any major decisions for at least a year.
- Be very careful about who you trust. Lean on those who love you.
- Spend time with family and friends but also give yourself "me time".

"...we are forced to reinvent our lives when a loved one dies..." –Leo Babauta
--Karen Gurney

After considering all that was hard once caregiving ended, I narrowed it down to learning how to slow down and plan for the future not just the present. The last years of Callum's life were spent planning in three-month increments. When an opportunity came along to have fun, do something we hadn't done or check off a bucket list item, I did everything possible to make it happen. There wasn't going to be another chance.

That thought pattern became a habit, and two years after caregiving I am finally able to plan more than three months ahead. This has come at an emotional, physical and financial cost. I built a house and completed some incredible personal and professional development training. All of it has made a huge difference in my life and I don't regret doing it. I really could have made it a two- or three-year plan instead of a fourteen-month one! I still functioned on the premise of "if you want it, you better do it now!" I had lost the ability to strategically plan my future.

Finding my own support team has been crucial in my transition from being a wife and caregiver to being single. Learning to give myself permission to take care of myself by bringing on board a counselor, personal trainer, massage therapist, chiropractor and having the courage to face the pain of the grief and loss were all key pieces to my recovery puzzle. Each one helped in their own way. I had met women who were very bitter, sad and angry years after losing their husband. I set a clear intention to not live the rest of my life that way.

The best thing someone can do when the caregiving has ended is to give themselves lots of time to recover. The physical recovery most likely will just start to happen as the body takes advantage of the opportunity to sleep and rest. The emotional recovery can be harder to deal with. I would highly recommend finding a method and support person to help uncover and release the pain. It will take time to work through all the layers and is so important to creating a new life. I want other former caregivers to know and believe that life will be good again. It will never be the same, but they will be able to enjoy life again.

Today I have a life full of opportunities and joy. I miss my husband every day and am grateful to have many happy memories. I have coped by being busy and been successful at doing that for over two years. That has not always served me well. I am closer to enjoying living a life that is not a roller coaster filled with high stress and having to be on high alert every minute. Part of my personal recovery has been to resolve the guilt issues I had for the opportunities that have come into my life because my husband died. I willingly chose to admit these were issues I had to deal with and that has helped me learn to genuinely enjoy and be excited by the life I get to live now.

One surprising thing I noticed over these past two years is that it seems I was in a time warp for about five years. I have little recollection or accurate memory of world political news, popular music and musical performers, television shows or movies. I realize that I blocked out so many things, especially during those last three years and the first year or two after Callum passed away.

One of the other things I really noticed was how long it took our family to start to have a "normal" relationship again. We had become so used to that high-stress life and our need to be with each other every moment possible that we didn't know how not to do that.

Overall, I am still working on finding the balance of living in peace, joy and hope, making each moment count, and doing it within reason and with responsibility. I fully believe in living my life with passion and following my dreams. The real learning has been to make a realistic plan to do it.
--Lorna M. Scott, speaker, trainer, coach and author of *Walking the Journey Together…Alone, Finding Peace, Hope and Joy in the Middle of the Sh***

The hardest time for me after caregiving ended was the emotional aspect of missing my parents (they were my care receivers) and the physical aspect of things going from crazy busy to nothing…just like that. One would think that if, as caregivers, we pray for the craziness to stop, we would be happy when it does. I went through things like keeping my mom's oxygen machine on just to hear it a little while longer to just closing my eyes in the silence. So, the new-found time was hard for me to deal with as was the grief. The two go hand-in-hand. It was also hard to still feel a sense of overwhelm with all that post caregiving required but without the caregiving. For example, I was their executor so I was busy keeping up with different kinds of paperwork.

It may sound odd but welcoming my feelings was very helpful. Whatever showed up for me, I allowed to be. It also helped me tremendously that I was so thankful for my time with my parents and we were complete and at peace with each other. My kids were very helpful, too.

Humor was a must! Funny shows, movies and sharing laughs and memories about my parents was very helpful. Also, taking time to spend with myself and learning to find myself again after all the time spent doing for others was critical. So, welcoming family, humor, taking time for myself and reengaging with the world helped.

I would offer several pieces of advice:
1. Welcome your feelings and know what you feel is exactly where you need to be and it's okay.
2. Put yourself first. Be gentle with yourself through this transitions. It's okay to be selfish!
3. Go somewhere with a friend, journal, take time for yourself. Do something that you enjoy.
4. Know that all your feelings will pass and you are NOT alone.

My life today is quiet. Sorry, had to throw that in. It's drama- and trauma-free. It's a welcome feeling from the years full of drama.

I found that friends who thrived on drama suddenly became cold and distant. At first I was hurt that people who were there for me and loved listening to the drama, who offered comfort and respite, were suddenly not there when things were good.

I am good. Life is good. I am moving forward with my life and friends who are there for me during the bad times and the good times. I am deeply passionate about family caregiving and supporting caregivers through the caregiving process. I want caregivers to avoid the mistakes I made and have the tools to turn their experience into greater peace and make the transitions through the stages of care smoother for all.
--Tandy Elisala, family caregiver coach and grief coach and author of *Healing Through the Chaos: Practical Care Giving*

Three Years

The hardest time for me was the days and weeks immediately after. I was completely numb. Sunshine, exercise, books, music and a few select people helped me most.

Take as much time as you need to heal. No one can tell you how much time you need. Period. The length of time a caregiver may need to heal depends on many factors. Caregivers benefit from customized solutions. If able to do so, allow someone proven to be trustworthy and who has the capacity to do so to care for you for a time. The best general advice given to me was from Sara Feigenholtz (D, Illinois House of Representatives, 12th District): "The biggest decision you need to make now is whether you want chocolate or vanilla ice cream."

My life today is changing. I see a definite need for a President's Committee on active family caregiving and a one-stop resource for aftergiving needs. I have yet to find a job resource center dedicated to caregivers re-entering the workforce.
--Janice Goldman

The hardest part of my caregiving journey was watching someone I love deteriorate so quickly, and knowing there was nothing I could do but be his advocate for the best care possible while trying to manage his symptoms.

Hospice saved my sanity. They allowed me to become a wife, a companion and a part of the end-of-life process without being his primary caregiver. I was able to let go of that weight and trust that someone else was able to take control of his physical state. I was fortunate to handle his fragile emotional state without the added burden of medication schedules, bathing, seizures and the like.

After my period of caregiving was over, after my husband's death, the hardest part was putting one foot in front of the other. I had two small children who could not possibly understand the finality of death when I couldn't quite grasp it myself. I sought help when I needed it. And I sought it often. I had days when I would do nothing but cry, days where grief sucker-punched me on an otherwise beautiful day. I had angry days. Content days. Unremarkable days.

And after a while, those days turned into years.

Three years later, it still stings. My oldest daughter still hurts. I still put one foot in front of the other. I cry. I laugh. I can look at pictures and remember cherished moments and appreciate them for the time in our life that was captured. Time doesn't heal all wounds, but it does sting less frequently and less harshly.
I believe we all have bruises from life, things that hurt us, things that change us into the beings we are capable of becoming. My bruises, however unfortunate, have helped others. People ask me for advice regarding their ill loved ones and I can help. I can offer advice because I have been there. I can offer hope because I survived.

My advice to others at the end of their caregiving journey is to be gentle to themselves. Allow time to heal. Don't second guess your choices or decisions. We do what we feel is best at the time, and you have to leave it there. Take care of yourself, because you are important too. Make time to soothe your soul. Death is an all-consuming process and the wounds do not heal themselves quickly or wholly.

This journey has put me on a different path altogether. I've found love, which I wasn't even looking for at the time. My children are older and wiser, sweeter and more tender than before.

I am back in college. I currently work as a Certified Nurse Assistant and aid an elderly patient several times a week. I am currently studying to be a Certified Medical Assistant and will finish the program next summer. After that, I will pursue nursing school. This is definitely not how I planned for my story to unfold but I know my experience will help others in some way. I am following my heart and remaining grateful for the opportunity to better myself in the settling dust of such unfortunate circumstances.

There is life after caregiving ends. And I owe it to myself to live it fully, without regrets.
--Skye Lanford

It is difficult to say exactly what was the most difficult time after caregiving was over. Each day, month, and year has its own challenges. I would say, however, that the first year and a half or so was the most difficult. As challenging as caregiving proved to be, it did give my life purpose and meaning. It was my role, so to speak, for four and a half years. So after my husband's death I had to learn to redefine my role and purpose in my life. I also struggled with the grief of losing my husband of over 39 years. Then finally I struggled with the "if only's," the "what if's," and the false guilt of the uncontrollable.

What helped me the most was my faith. I went deep into God's Word, and leaned heavily on God. I still do. It is essential for my well-being. I began to realize too that my identity was not based on the roles I had played in my life. Roles are entirely different than one's identity. First of all my identity and purpose was found in the Lord. But I was an unique individual and personality within that framework.

Grief from the loss of a dear loved one never leaves one entirely. To think otherwise is naive. The grief greatly softens, and joy can return. One must come to a point of acceptance for this to happen. Yet as I said before, it never leaves completely. It becomes a part of whom one becomes. That is not all bad, as it can be a vehicle of compassion and help in someone else's life. For awhile I struggled with the concept of leaving what is behind and reaching for the new goals God has/had in my future. I came to understand that our caregiving pasts help to mold our futures, and that is a good thing.

As to what I would advise caregivers adjusting to life after caregiving, I would say be kind and gentle with yourself. You are going to go through a period of deep grief especially if the person you lost was someone you deeply loved. Know too that you don't have to figure out what should be your next step or role in life right away. Think deeply about this, and take your time. I found personally I needed to draw very closely to the Lord in this process. Also don't engage in the guilt thing. No caregiver was ever a perfect caregiver. I found that I needed to acknowledge and release these things to the Lord. Much guilt we feel, however, is false guilt about things that were beyond our control. We need to let that go also. We also need to remember that feelings do not equal truth.

As to my life today, it is good. I will always miss my husband. Also there is unique challenges

with being a widow. There are times when I still fight loneliness, and just facing life's issues are somewhat more difficult alone. Yet as I said before my faith has deepened, and I have grown in so many ways as a person through the difficulties of caregiving and my days as a widow.
--Sharon Vander Waal

The death of a family member is a very difficult time for everyone involved. Additionally, someone who was close to the departed in a caregiving role may have some very confusing emotions to deal with.

When my first wife passed, the caregiving aspect of our relationship didn't immediately affect me. For the first week or so, I was staying with her parents because I simply could not be alone. Because the situation was so intense and new at the time, caregiving was the last thing on my mind. All I really knew at any point in time was whether it was light or dark outside, or if I had to go to the bathroom.

After the first week, I returned home to a very empty house. My employer told me to take as much time as I needed, so I had no pressing responsibilities. Just a lot of empty time. This was the first time I felt that something was "off." At the regularly scheduled medication and caregiving times, I started going through the motions of preparing meds or getting the trach care tray ready. Then I stopped myself because there wasn't anyone there to whom I could administer these things.
After a week of doing this, it struck me - I don't have to do these things any longer! I boxed up all of the remaining medical supplies so that I would stop going through the motions. At some point during that week, I realized that I now have three hours every day that I didn't have before. And I was ecstatically happy about this! But that didn't feel right. One of the worst things that can happen to someone happened to me, and there was some aspect of it that made me happy and relieved. I felt guilty because I shouldn't be feeling happy now, should I?

There was another aspect of this situation that made it worse. We had been together for about nine years. But the last five or so years were not good for us; right before she got sick, we were basically roommates. The only reason we were still together was because I didn't want to look like the jerk who kicked the disabled girl out of his house. (She had a disability before she got sick.) When she was in the hospital, at first I wanted to walk away from the whole situation because we didn't have anything between us. But I couldn't just abandon her, so I stuck around. After she was released into my care, I started to feel what I thought was a deeper love for her. But in retrospect, this was most likely a feigned emotion, something my mind created to justify my continuing care for her. After her passing I had two burdens lifted off of my shoulders: first, the caregiving role; second, the fact that I was no longer trapped in a bad relationship. This made the guilt worse, but it also made the happiness and relief more intense.

I worked through these emotions as I worked through my grief. About four weeks after her passing I returned to work, and got back into my daily routine. The first few days of this were somewhat jarring. Because I had changed my frame of mind and daily routine to "this is what we do every day during the week, we drive to work, do work, then drive home", I had put the "I don't have to do this medication and trach care" fact out of mind. So for the first few days, I'd come home, put my things in the closet, and go right to the cabinet with the meds.

Of course, the meds weren't there. It took me a week or so to get used to this new daily routine without the caregiving aspects. At that time, I began going to a monthly widower support group, which helped immensely.

My biggest challenge during this time was staying true to myself. During times when I was happy, it felt wrong; I felt that I should force myself to feel sad. I would go read horrible news stories and watch terrible videos to force myself to feel sad. At some point during those first three weeks, I realized how counterproductive this was. It didn't feel good in the times after I had forced myself down this path; but in the times I had felt naturally sad, I did not get a bad feeling.

Once I realized that this "staying true to myself" was a problem, I set out to fix it. The best way to do this, as I found, is to mindfully immerse oneself in activity. I'm not talking about doing lots of things during all of one's waking hours in order to hide or not pay attention to one's grief. That is also counterproductive and can lead to a much longer recovery time. In my circumstance, I started doing mindful activities a couple of weeks after her passing. I made sure to give myself plenty of grief time but I also went out and immersed myself in activity during the right time.

Another term for this kind of immersion is mindfulness. One of my favorite activities was hiking in a local park. The first time I started down the trail, I had no idea exactly how big this park is. A few hours later, I realized that I was lost and, a few hours after that, I realized that I had no idea how to find my way. But I didn't have a care in the world. I was concentrating on the deep green color of the leaves of the trees, the fragrances of the wildflowers along the paths, the sound that the gentle breeze made as it worked its way across the tall grass.

When you concentrate on your senses and what is happening in the moment, you give your mind a chance to rest. The distracting thoughts, the preconceived notions about how you "should" feel, the stress of the situation all fall away and allow you to think with a clear mind.

In terms of caregiving, my life is better than it was during that time of my life. I am a caregiver for my current wife, who needs daily medication. However, we have help in the form of daily nursing and aide visits.
--Anonymous

Four Years

I would have to say there were a few times that may qualify as the hardest for me in different ways. First was immediately following my mom's death. I had to make a decision to intubate her again or not. Thus, to let her go. It was at the very moment my sister had left the hospital to go get some new clothes. I am an explorer and doubter of religion. Given the pain and suffering I watched my mom go through, I was very angry at God or the Universe for leaving me alone in that moment. After not being able to communicate for quite some time, I grabbed her a hand and asked her what she wanted. Something gave her the strength to grab me and I felt her nail in my hand, and I knew I had to let her go.

The hardest time for me after that was wondering if I made the right decision. What if she could have recovered? What if I made the wrong decision because I was so exhausted? What if I did things differently earlier, like gone to live with her and take care of her there, would this have happened? The doubt immediately following her death was horrible.

Later, as my grief processed, it was hard because I became angry at her. Angry at her for smoking for so long, giving her the COPD that ruined her quality of life in the end. Angry at her lying about her COPD diagnosis for years, telling us she had allergies. Angry at her for sneaking cigarettes even after her diagnosis. I felt horribly guilty for feeling anger toward my dear mother who was now gone and who had suffered so much. The feelings of "what if" were, and sometimes still are, torture.

Another difficulty was that no one ever acknowledged the difficulty I had in making that decision. Not one of my family members. I know they all suffered the pain of her loss, took care of her and went through their own grief process. But I felt, and sometimes still do, feel alone on an island of doubt. Did they hate me for it? Love me for it? Feel bad I was there alone or grateful they weren't? Did they give a shit at all?

My advice for someone after caregiving is to care for yourself. No matter what, without guilt. The whole idea of taking care of yourself so you can take better care of others is true. But I doubt any caregiver going through a traumatic event with a loved one is taking much time for meditation, or massage, or even a few good hours of sleep for that matter. Do that now. You deserve it. You need it, and your loved one wants that for you.

The caregiving process and end of that process changes you, your family, and that dynamic. It could be for the better or for the worse. Don't allow that to impact your beliefs about yourself. You did everything in your power, from love, and took on a task that many never have to face.

Today I have come to terms with my decision. I believe in the messages I received, my dedication to my mother, and the appreciation she had for our journey together following my father's death and leading up to hers. I have more appreciation and patience for people. Everyone has their own journey and pain they may be dealing with.

It has changed what I define as success, happiness, and what is important in life, and driven me to live according to my true self.
--Sue Koch, owner, Soaring Solutions

The first year was awful. I felt guilty for not having taken time off through Family Medical Leave Act and just not spending enough time with my grandfather and family. I felt lost, apathetic and unmotivated--feelings which I had only experienced once before when dealing with a tough break-up. But this time, I felt lost in a different way, and I think it had to do with what my job was at the time. I was working for the Alzheimer's Association at the time and instead of feeling comforted or inspired by that, I just wanted to completely stop thinking about and being surrounded by or reminded of Alzheimer's. I wanted to get rid of all my "purple" Alzheimer's stuff, and just separate myself from the eldercare world entirely, a world which had been my passion and career focus for years. I think that's what was hardest--wondering if I'd ever be able to enjoy talking about, advocating for and working in eldercare again.

Time helped me most.

Let yourself experience every emotion, good and bad, that comes with the grief process after caregiving ends. Be vulnerable. Be honest about your feelings--with yourself and with others. Seek what you can learn from the process and how it can change you in a positive way, a way you never imagined it could or would.

My life today is more balanced, focused and free. Free of fear--fear of saying no, fear of not being perfect.
--Michelle Seitzer

Five Years

The hardest time for me after caregiving ended was reconnecting with friends and making new ones. I had isolated myself or avoided taking my father to public gatherings so I had to reconstruct my social life again.

I also lost my sense of purpose for awhile, but was thankful to have my website (www.intentionalcaregiver.com/) to continue to work on.

Just as during my caregiving experience, my family was not helpful after my father passed. Everything fell upon me. They did come to pay their last respects about a month before his passing but were not there when he passed and did not help to make decisions after his passing. My mother assumed that I would drive from Idaho to California to deliver things to my siblings that they had asked for, such as large tools, lawnmowers, dressers, etc. (as if I had the money and time). She was actually very rude to me for several years, feeling that I could just drop everything and play delivery girl or retrieve money from trusts at whim. (My mother was never legally divorced from my father so technically everything belonged to her but she had not lived with him for eight years.)

One of the very hardest things was closing the guardianship/conservatorship. It requires getting all records and then showing up in court to be discharged from the title. Very sad and very lonely.

My 90-year-old mother will be coming to live with me (yes, despite her rudeness) and this time, things will be different because I anticipate that she will be difficult. I'll set limits. I'll call in home care help rather than stumbling through all the caregiving myself. I will take MUCH more away time for myself. I will give my siblings an ultimatum that either her money is spent on home care help (and they will sign something) or I'll refuse to be the caregiver.

Life today is filled with more freedom, of course, but mostly it is filled with less worry. Because of my father's dementia and mobility/instability issues, I never knew what he would do next. He refused to sit around and was therefore prone to falls. There were continuous battles over use of dangerous tools and I never could figure out a way of selling them without being disrespectful.

But then again, I look around and see things that remind me of him. His canes are still kept in the antique butter churn. I still keep his special coffee cup in the pantry. When the geese return to our pond and raise another batch of goslings, I think, Awwwwww, Dad would have loved to have seen this.
--Shelley Webb

The hardest time after caregiving ended was finding a purpose in my life. My whole life has been about my children. Helping with Heather's care during her cancer was part of being her mother. For 24 years, I had cared for her and every illness. Now there was a void. My daughter was gone, my caring for her well-being was ended. I felt like I had stepped into a bottom-less pit.

My best advice I can give is to try and find a way to fill your time with purpose. I used my time to do some things I had never done and wanted to do to keep busy. I took painting and cake decorating classes. I enjoyed new hobbies, but felt I still was needed elsewhere. I decided to start a non-profit organization in my community to create ovarian cancer awareness. I've met new friends, created a new meaning in my life and have something new to wake up to everyday.

My life today is filled with passion to create a lasting legacy in memory of Heather and to make a difference in the world. Nothing will completely heal my loss, but I feel that I can help others with cancer and help other caregivers. I have a deep understanding of what being a caregiver is, and how your whole family changes when someone is put into that role. Through our cancer advocacy, and reaching out, we hope we help others to heal as well.
--Frieda Weeks, Founder, Hope for Heather

When my mother-in-law died, a friend wrote to me offering sympathy and also tentatively suggesting that it was okay to feel relief as well as grief. I had little time to feel anything during the rush of things that needed to be done in the days and weeks after death. I expected that grief would come to me suddenly, unexpectedly--but it never did in any big ways. Months later, there was still only relief. I had my life back.

The hardest time for me after caregiving ended may well have been the settling of my mother-in-law's estate--specifically, deciding what to do with boxes and boxes of fairly valuable stuff. I gave away what I could to friends and relatives--even shipped six large UPS cartons to Florida to extended family there, and still there was so much left over. One day, determined to deal with the stuff, I filled my minivan to the gills with decorative plates, hand-painted bowls, tea sets, and more. I drove from antique shop to antique shop in Dallas-Forth Worth and sold one beautiful bowl for $15. Nobody wanted the precious treasures my mother-in-law (and her mother before her) had spent her life collecting. Mind you, I have boxes of stuff put away for each of my daughters and more in use around the house. I know I'm not the only one who is overwhelmed by the decisions left to us after a loved one dies and their treasures become clutter to the rest of the world.

So I donated. In doing so, I felt both release and guilt. I must have donated thousands of dollars worth of stuff--but is it really worth anything when no one wants to buy it? Someone has to make the decisions. I did the best I could.

My word to those whose loved ones have died is exactly what my friend said to me. You may grieve, or not. Surely you will feel relief, too, and that's okay. Feel what you feel -- even if it's nothing.

My life today is absolutely blessed, which is not to say perfect or without trials. A danger for me during the caregiving years was thinking that after my mother-in-law died I would be free and all would be well. I'm more free, that is certain, but my kids still get sick and need me and things still break and go wrong and the world still falls apart around me at times. Most of my parents' health woes are still ahead of them, and I have no idea what that will look like--but I know it will come. Younger members of the family may need short-term or extended care. Even though one season of caregiving is behind me, I am sure there are more seasons of hardship still ahead. And while I can't say I'm excited about that, I don't dread it like I used to. I'm grateful for a season to focus on my marriage, parenting, career, and artistic pursuits. The hardship of caregiving makes me appreciate this season of freedom, and for that I'm strangely grateful.
--Lisa Ohlen Harris, author of *The Fifth Season, A Daughter-in-Law's Memoir of Caregiving*

Six Years

My aunt died a week ago. Yesterday evening, the church choir I sing with presented a beautiful All Souls Day requiem service to commemorate deceased loved ones and "all the faithful departed." I thought about my parents and in-laws who have passed away. Like so many people today, they lived with conditions like macular degeneration, cancer, COPD, stroke, Parkinson's, and Alzheimer's.

Last night at church I thought of them with much gratitude, and some sadness. But the intense grief is over. When my mom died in September 2007, the last of that generation was gone, and 20 years of caregiving came to a close. The months immediately following her death were the hardest time for me because of my deep feelings of loss. I grieved that I could no longer hold Mom in my arms, share my life with her, give her a kiss, sing with her, have dinner with her. It broke my heart to know I'd never see her again.

Beyond losing Mom, I also lost the meaning and satisfaction I felt as a caregiver. The important help I gave was no longer needed. I didn't need to console, support, or fly to Chicago to provide respite. After caregiving ended, the crucial decisions were over. I was proud to help make some life-and-death choices, and happy to, in some small way, repay my parents for all they'd given me. It surprised me but I was sad to see the caregiving journey end.

Looking back on my caregiving years, I have no regrets. I was actively involved and tried to help in a loving way over all the years when my family needed care. I wasn't perfect in my attitudes, actions or reactions. I made mistakes and wasn't always a happy giver, but I was faithful. I gave it my best and I gave it my all. Knowing I was there for them, despite the difficulties, really helped me get through my feelings of loss.

With active caregiving behind me, and after grieving the loss of those I loved, I looked for ways to reinvest my energy. Caregiving helped me learn and grow. It opened my eyes to see many facets of the caregiving experience. It opened my ears to hear caregivers' subtle, yet profound expressions of loss and suffering. It planted in my heart a desire to care for caregivers.

So, in 2008 I began a new type of caregiving journey. I founded a company called Partners on the Path to help caregivers preserve their health, resilience and capacity to care. This is a new way to experience the satisfaction and meaning of caregiving.
--Jane Meier Hamilton, author of *The Caregiver's Guide to Self-Care: Help for Your Caregiving Journey*

The hardest time was a combination of missing my father and reliving the experience and thinking about what I would have done differently. When you are in the middle of caring for a loved one you have to make the best decisions you can at the time. However, afterward it is very easy to be a Monday morning quarterback and question your decisions and choices. I have talked with other caregivers and this is very common.

Speaking to my wife, family and friends helped me most. I was fortunate because caregiving did not rip our family apart and after my father died we all supported each other. Everyone in my life was incredibly supportive, especially Susan, my wife, and reminded me of all the things I did right. Also we found out that Susan was pregnant a month after my father died so that helped ease the pain. We saw it as the cycle of life - one family member leaves and another one arrives. All of our children are special but our daughter, Avery, played an especially important role in our life considering the timing of her conception and birth.

You will always miss the loved one. I think about my father every day. That is natural and don't be upset by it. Also, have no regrets. Most caregivers do the best they can under the circumstances and that is really all we can do.

Overall I am very happy. However, caregiving changed me. It helped give me focus and made me want to share my experience with other so they can avoid the mistakes we made which is why we created eCareDiary. Caregiving also helped prepare me for being a parent myself. It taught me patience and also how to multitask, two things you need with young children.

My father was fortunate to see four of his seven grandchildren but I wish he had met our children and his only granddaughter, Avery. That is my only regret but clearly this was something not in my control so I don't lose sleep over it.
--John Mills, co-founder of eCareDiary.com

The hardest time for me, after my caree died, was the first couple of years. It took me a long time to find my identity. Soon after my mom's death I volunteered to give companionship to dementia and Alzheimer's sufferers at Leeza's Place while their family caregivers attended the support group. I needed to fill a hole within me and I thought continuing to be a caregiver would help. I thoroughly enjoyed the experience and fell in love with my new carees, but I still felt lost. After a year I decided to stay with a friend in Italy. Maybe I was running away from the rubble that was my life at the time. I spent a year in Italy, during which time I wrote my book.

What helped me the most was starting my life over in a new area, getting a new job, and enjoying my free time in leisure activities. In other words, distancing myself from caregiving. Although writing mine and my mother's story was cathartic, promoting it, joining caregiver organizations, as well as the Alzheimer's Associations, fundraising, and writing articles about the subject kept caregiving on my mind. So, I took a break. I prayed and meditated, got a fun part time job doing demos in Sam's Club, and now I do the things I enjoy in my free time.

My life now is tranquil. My husband and I spend our free time exploring the area that we live and doing the things we like, sometimes together, other times separately. We spend as much time as possible with our families, too. I continue to support caregiving organizations financially and/or physically but with a happy heart. It doesn't control me anymore.
--Emily Placido, author of *Julita's Sands, a Memoir*

Seven Years

The hardest time was when memory of his last moment came alive. He suffered in great pain in front of my eyes because of what the U.S. healthcare has/hasn't done. I thought about it every day and couldn't forget for a very long time. Another hard times were job interviews. Many asked what motivated me to become a pharmacist and I had to explain my long journey. I couldn't help buy cry...I cried almost at every possible interview.

I share my personal story whenever I can so people can be aware and that has helped me the most. I am also part of an organization called Victims of Medical Errors and cope with others who were hurt by medical errors. We work on projects together and discuss improvements of the healthcare system. So I would recommend doing what I am doing. Share your story although it hurts and is private. No one will know or forget how much you and your loved one has suffered if you don't share.

I work as a pharmacist and consult with patients and help out with medications. I especially strive to find solutions for patients with limited English proficiency because it is so easy for them--more than people who can speak English--to fall in healthcare gaps.
--Soojin Jun

When Father Orlando took his last breath, it was surreal. His breathing patterns had been changing rapidly the last 90 minutes of his life but nothing really prepares you for when the transition happens. You cry, you laugh, you rejoice and, immediately, you start to reminisce.

Preparing to leave the hospital after his transition to eternal life was no different than some of the other nights I had left the hospital when he was still alive. I always had personal belongings to shuttle back and forth from the hospital, just as I did the night he died. Walking out of the hospital at 1:30 a.m. that early Friday morning, I remember I had a strange sensation run through my body. The sensation was and still is difficult to explain but something that is etched in my memory. Recognizing that I would never have to return to the hospital to visit him again created an immediate void in my routine.

The next few days planning the trip back to Rochester, N.Y., for the funeral mass and burial was very similar to being his caregiver. I was making all the plans; he was going along for the ride! He always liked it that way. Working through the wake and funeral mass was therapeutic. Yet it was precisely at the burial site when I recognized that my caregiving duties had ended. When the final prayer was recited and we headed back to our cars, I remember looking back at his coffin while saying to myself, "I guess I'm not needed anymore."

Arriving at the airport the day after the burial to return to Florida was the hardest time for me. It was at this time that it hit me square in the eye that he was gone, that my caregiving duties were finished and both of our lives changed in ways we really don't fully understand. This was also when the grieving process started. His life transition changed both of us. I was leaving him behind, and moving on with my life in uncharted waters. Eighteen years of friendship solidified by 18 months of intense in-home caregiving only made our bond stronger. There were many difficult caregiving days during our 18 months together in Florida, but there was never a more difficult day than getting on that plane in Rochester and flying solo to Florida without him.

During the last month that Father Orlando spent in our condominium, we had the opportunity to talk openly about so many different things that happened in our lives. Yet there was a moment during this time when he looked at me and said, "I know you are going to be devastated when I die, but please know that I have had a good life and know that you have made me very happy." Those words still ring in my ear, and I know how fortunate I am to have him speak those words to me, especially since he was unable to communicate the last 72 hours of his life.

When the experience of death was still raw, it was hard to find immediate comfort in those words because I missed his physical presence. As time passed, his words that day provided me the ability to learn to get to know him in a different way. I still miss him; rather, I miss his physical presence. Those words that he spoke that day are forever etched in my memory. Gone but never forgotten, here but not physically present. His words that day were the greatest gift that he ever gave me.

The biggest lesson that I had to learn, unfortunately, I had to learn the hard way. Make sure that any decisions you make are not made out of your emotions. While we all grieve differently, grief will play tricks on your emotions and change your decision-making process. At first you do not recognize this change but it does happen. You make decisions based on what you think the person you are grieving for would want you to make. It is a slippery slope but it is also can be a dangerous and expensive slope if not recognized early in the process.

Decisions based on emotions often turn disastrous. Embrace your grief, share it with those with whom you feel most comfortable and do not be afraid to cry. Trust someone to care for you while being open about your fears and concerns. Having a trusted confident during the grieving process will help take away some of the emotional burden. It is during those times when our emotions are raw when poor decisions are made.

Being Father Orlando's caregiver for the last 18 months of his life solidified our friendship, and brought a beautiful sunset to his life. Now seven years since his transition to eternal life, I find myself still missing him, yet knowing him in a different way. The 18 months of caregiving for Father Orlando taught both of us the true meaning of love, trust, commitment and loyalty. I know life's journeys are not often driven on smooth roads but we can always hope for a gentle wind at our back. Those gentle winds are often solidified by love, trust, commitment, and loyalty. We both learned the true meanings of those words during our caregiving journey, which continues to have a profound effect on my life today.
--Chris MacLellan

Eleven Years

The hardest time was undoubtedly getting through the immediate aftermath of my husband's dying and all the arrangements, formal funeral, extended family visits, immediate family issues, death certificate, insurance policies, ad infinitum. I was deadly tired/exhausted, and prayed constantly that I could just "get through this." I never objected to the mass of details in caregiving, but after caregiving turned out to be much more than I had bargained for. I now understand why so many of my friends/associates are postponing the memorial service until months after their loved one's death. One needs time to recoup and recharge the batteries.

What helped me most? I would have to say TIME. It may be a bit of a cliche, but "time heals all wounds" was certainly true for me. Each month I felt less raw, and more able to create and re-vision a life for myself. My spiritual life was a key to keeping my sanity and emotions in order. Close friends, with whom I could laugh and share a glass of wine, proved to be so life-affirming.

Stay in touch with friends, reach out for your needs, have a plan to recoup your energies and life flow, but don't expect a support system to just magically show up. False expectations--we want our children or close friends to take care of us--will lead to disappointment and resentment. It's important to take time for yourself and assess your new situation carefully. Do your inner work through prayer, meditation and/or therapy. Group support can be a help, but not always. One of my friends went to a monastery after his wife died. He found that very peaceful. Another woman friend took that Santiago, St. James walk in Spain for two months. She met marvelous friends and took on an entirely new lease on life. She was also one who postponed the memorial from February to the following June after her energy and strength returned. She spent many months in semi-solitude, very low-key, before the memorial, as well.

I must also confess that I resumed my university teaching after one term on leave of absence. It felt normal and natural for me to be back in the classroom with young people, whose energy and vivacity can ignite anyone! I did not leave my environment at all, but learned to take advantage of everything that was available to heal my body and soul.

(My life today is) beautiful. Serene and joyful. Two years after Jim died I met a lovely man and we married the following April, honeymooned in Spain and now continue to be very active with my family mainly, our community, his music/my writing and teaching. We have a host of friends, live in a lovely neighborhood, garden intensively, host an international student on a regular basis, and otherwise find our lives just a bit busy from time to time (understatement). We spend January and part of February in Mexico enjoying the absence of phone, schedules and Northwest Pacific rainy winters. Quite restful, actually, and always enjoyable to be in a warm climate with such hospitable people as the Mexicans invariably are.

Guilt may assail the newly released caregiver, and it can come with a punch. You're sitting back, relaxed, enjoying yourself with family and/or friends, and suddenly, you feel as though you're betraying your loved one who suffered so and no longer is there to share your life with you.

These and other negative emotions can undo your best efforts to create a life for yourself that is meaningful for you. This is when you will find spirituality to be such a healing process.

Spirituality is a very significant feature of life after caregiving, however a person defines and practices it. I have also found giving--with money, time, or other means to family, friends, charity, good causes, even beggars, etc--to be very healing, as it makes you aware of your connection with all other humans, regardless of their age, gender, ethnicity, country of origin and other so-called differences.

Above all, count your blessings moment by moment. Look around you at the enormous abundance in your life and smile joyfully. My husband, Burl, who is a charming storyteller, always says: "May you have the things you love, and may you love the things you have." With this motto, you will never be without everything you need.
--Nanette J. Davis, Ph.D., author of *The ABCs of Caregiving: Words to Inspire You* and *Caregiving Our Loved Ones: Stories and Strategies That Will Change Your Life*

After almost 12 years what I remember most are specific moments.

I had to leave a grocery store because a young couple was bickering about nothing I deemed important and they didn't recognize the preciousness of life.

There was no magic prize (the return of John) at Day 366 and everybody said I just had to make it through the first year.

When I sold our car and, later, our house to conserve money--both for the technical and emotional nature of the work.

When a CD or movie he would have liked came out and he didn't get to see it.

The people who met me as I was in that moment. Some days I really just wanted to talk about TV shows, some days I wanted to tell stories of my life with John, sometimes I was just super hungry and was grumpy because of that and not because I was mourning. My existence wasn't completely John when I was a caregiver, and wasn't completely about grief after he died. The people who continued to travel with me were my safety net and salvation. My gratitude for the men who saw me the first Friday night after John died...as I quietly tried to have a "regular" Friday and who met me with open smiles set the tone for my healing and I will never forget them.

Some people wanted me to grieve the way they imagined I would (I usually disappointed them), some people thought that they needed to win the grief Olympics (none of them were his family, who were the only people who could have been contenders).

The "wait a year before you do anything important" is not worth thinking about. Stuff needs to get done, and in the first year society still is willing to deal with people in mourning as if they were dressed in black (something I actually will do more of when I enter mourning again at some point in my life). If your gut was trustworthy before, it likely still is. If you will lose money on a house you can no longer afford just because it hasn't been a year, then find a condo and sell the house. It can be scary to be fully in charge of (and responsible for) your own life without the trusted adult counsel of a spouse, but start with small stuff and just keep moving forward on the time line that feels right.

I have married again and have a 5-year-old son. Unlike a lot of my young widow(er) peers I continue to have a deep and meaningful relationship with my first in-laws. They love my husband and son and welcomed them easily.

My career, the state I live in, and my home life are all very different than the months before I became a caregiver and the time immediately after John died. My life is good, but not any more smooth or gentle than anybody else's life is. The days of mourning are usually just a day or two now, instead of weeks at a time. I still get mad, every once in awhile, at the people who have had less obvious turmoils. I imagine their lives to not have these deep aches but I know that is just my imagination. Nobody comes fully into their adulthood without aches, if they are obvious to outsiders simply doesn't matter. I'm okay, it took about five years before I felt fully myself again, but I'm okay.
--Heather Campbell Furtek Slutzky

Twelve Years

After caregiving ended, I was left feeling a huge responsibility for Loretta's three kids, two girls, ages 8 and 10, and a boy, 14. Their father, who had long been overwhelmed by life at best, a mental case at worst, would only become more so as they grew up. I came to be a part-time caregiver early on when he was unable to take my sister to chemo and radiation because he had had cancer himself and just "couldn't" do it. Good grief, I thought, get with the effing program. So I drove her to and from chemo and radiation for years (she got diagnosed in 1994 and died in 2001). In an ironic twist, since her husband had had cancer before they got married, I remember my mother being worried Loretta would be left a widow. Hah.

More than anything else, I would tell someone not to try to do it themselves. Get a professional or use multiple strictly enforced shifts of family and friends as caregivers. In her last couple of months, her husband insisted on doing it all himself and didn't sleep, didn't eat, etc., and became filled with psychoses that we were then saddled with. He asked me to help him after she had horrible end-stage diarrhea. My sister and life-long best friend was laying there unconscious, naked and soiled and I was forced into helping. It was an effing horror show, but I think it was meant to be heroic. And none of my family, including our mother, had ever been through this and didn't know that this wasn't the way it was supposed to go. Loretta's husband became just another thing to worry about for everyone else. The selfish thing is to try to do it alone; it appears to be a selfless idea, but it's not. He was at it 24/7 while we all took breaks to go to work, etc., and it totally overwhelmed his already-tenuous grip on mental stability.

The only help I remember except for the hospice nurse who came by just to check vitals and prescriptions was a social worker who gathered Loretta's kids around her bed and had a discussion about open versus closed casket—would they like to see her one last time or "remember her as she was". That was mind-bending to me. It was painful but necessary and not a choice that I was ever given as a kid.

One day she turned to me out of the blue and asked, "What do you think of cremation?" I said, Whatever you want. Why are you asking after having chosen a wake? "Formaldehyde." Again, I told her to do whatever she wanted. I only realized later that she didn't want to make more decisions, but wanted somebody to take responsibility for those kinds of things for her. She didn't bring it up again, and I wish I had taken it as more than sort of unnerving death talk.

One particularly bad event was when she had been comatose for days, was full of morphine, and apparently comfortable. One evening, her husband decided she had slid too far down in the bed and so decided it was important to pull her back up. He asked for my help. When we moved her, she woke up in what must have been horrific pain. At this point the cancer was in her spine, etc. He panics and flees, decides he needs to go out for coffee, not knowing what to do, I guess. I'm left with her looking up through her one open eye as she's trying to say something. Water? Morphine? All I could gather was "orrr". And me being so dense and saying to her, Oh, I wish I could understand you, Loretta. I finally figured out it was either water or morphine. She couldn't enunciate, but she wanted morphine. I think I would have given her the whole bottle a dropper at a time to send her back to where she had been, but it only took a little. So his kids had to see all this lunacy unfold in addition to their mother fading away in a hospital bed in the playroom. Later that night, he started telling anyone who would listen, "Kevin wants to nail me to the cross for hurting Loretta because I tried to move her." Again, no one is being done any kind of favor by a "selfless" overwhelmed solo caregiver.

The hardest thing to adjust to was to not feel her presence after she was finally gone. She has been dead 12 years and I've never felt like she is "around" or "looking down" or any of the other oft-used phrases. She was a spiritual person and I always thought I'd be able to "feel" her presence.

What helped me the most initially was that she had left a handwritten letter to the family to be found after she was gone. She wrote it about a year before she died, when she saw that the next decline would be something she wouldn't come back from. Basically, it was her wondering how she could possibly be happy after she was gone when she wouldn't be near her family until they died. She said that in the Bible it says that a day is like a thousand years and a thousand years like a day, and that it would seem very quick to her until we were together again. At the time, having this document that she wrote knowing she would already be gone when we saw it broke me down but made me happy, too. But I feel more and more as I get older that all this may be "all there is" and wonder if all of the afterlife talk is just to keep all of us from depression and a dread of dying. But, I often change my views about this on a daily basis.

Regarding Loretta, I am in contact with her kids and see them on holidays at my mother's house. All three made it successfully through college and now work. The youngest girl had adjustment/depression problems and we got her together with a therapist who helped. Again, this was left to me and my wife; her father just "allowed" it to happen. Loretta's husband died about a year ago after heart surgery, strokes, etc., all of which we had to suffer through with him since all he wanted out of life, it seemed, was sympathy.

I know I will never again watch something like that unfold (see a household go crazier and crazier from badly planned caregiving) and not do something about it. Since it wasn't my house, I didn't push too hard. Now, I would find some way to change things in the caregiving if I ever saw that again. The person most willing to take on the caregiving may be the least able.

I also had never had someone die at home before, and that part actually came peacefully when everyone else was asleep or passed out and it wasn't creepy like I had always imagined. My mom would tell stories of all the wakes being at her house when she was little and the body being there when she would get up at night, and my little mind was totally freaked out. Now, whether it's me or someone else doing the dying, I would want it to be at home if possible.
--Kevin Lisankie

Fourteen Years

My mom was diagnosed with metastatic breast cancer in January 1998. From that time forward, she was unable to live in her own home. Her immediate needs moved her into my residence with my husband and myself.

During that time, my house was full of activity and, in spite of this monster that consumed my mom in front of my eyes, for the most part it was a wonderful time.

My mom's close friends and siblings would come visit from time to time and would toward the end chip in to help with household duties like cooking, and "babysitting" for Mom while I stepped out. My sister Heidi became a mother her first and second time during Mom's illness, so having babies around was also (obviously) a wonderful distraction. We had several family reunions at my home, and it proved to be a wonderful time to reconnect with cousins, aunts and uncles.

I also had several outside sources of communication during my caregiving years; a close group of friends that I met daily at a specific time and place; a counselor who I could tell ANYTHING and did; and a community band I was a member of that allowed me to free myself of the day-to-day stresses of caregiving.

I also had a great deal of my mother's medical personnel to turn to with questions--and I asked LOTS of questions. There were a few people who came to the house for quick blood work or med checks.

At the end, hospice played an integral part in both my mother's and my life; people came almost daily for the last two months of her life.

But, I was still tied to Mom with a cellphone (enormous in size, compared to those now) and a pager; those were the constants in my life.

There were also ongoing stresses in my marriage, which had been tedious for a few years before Mom moved in and the stresses compounded. Not unexpected.

When Mom died, literally all of that stopped.
My mother was gone.
My job of caregiving was done; the position vanished.
Mom's friends stopped calling and visiting.
My aunt and uncle stopped coming and the calls fell off to none.
My sister no longer needed to be at the house, so she stopped coming, which meant the babies stopped coming. That, next to losing Mom, hurt almost the worst.
The medical support stopped and any camaraderie I shared with them vanished.
My husband and I no longer had a "buffer" so I was not only thrown into this deep abyss of grief but also into the reality that my marriage had failed.

Mom's death left me not only a 40-something orphan, but it left me both emotionally and psychologically wounded as well as physically exhausted.

A year and change later, I left my husband for the incredible need for personal safety. I'd lost all the aforementioned things and now my marriage.

What DIDN'T help me was the fact that I'd isolated myself. I felt like all these people that had been in my life and moved on in their own and didn't need to be burdened with my silly drama.

I continued to deal with a counselor who helped me find my way and discovered many new things to do that "calmed" my mind like woodcarving and photography and, of course, music.

It's been 14 years since my mother died and there are days I still struggle.

I did a bit of volunteering for hospice; I NEEDED to feel NEEDED. I still reach out to people to help with time and talent or anything I can do. I'm especially drawn to fellow caregivers; I can almost pick them out of the crowd by their haunted, exhausted eyes.

My experience I don't suppose is typical; death and a divorce in a year but then I guess that leans heavily on the definition of "normal".

My advice is simple. Give yourself some grace. Take things (everything) one day at a time. Caregiving takes a toll on every system in your mind and body. Be good to yourself and don't try so hard to get back to that place you were before caregiving. You may never find it; so much has changed, including you, and you can't just "change" who you've become.

How do I describe my life today? There's a lot of truth in time heals! I'm something of a "late bloomer." I've taken some time in my life to discover who I am, and what my place in this life is. I've not remarried, and have no immediate plans to do so, either! As a person, I see myself as being a far more compassionate person than I was and have a seemingly infinite supply of patience. And, although it looked awfully dark all those years ago, my life now is bright and exciting.
--Gretchen Monteith

I remember, in the beginning, that the days seemed endless. My husband died on a Thursday, and every Thursday, I would think, I can't believe I've lived another week without him here. I feel like the adjustment happens one molecule at a time, it's that slow. Though I think when you live with the person you've lost, you're forced to understand they've died more quickly. Every single moment in your day has shifted with their absence – you no longer buy their brand of toothpaste at the store, you don't hear their steps on the porch around five o'clock, you only need to make coffee for one person rather than two. So for me my husband's absence kept hitting me hard with these small details.

I remember feeling incredibly alone, and yet disinterested, or maybe unable, to engage with my friends. What helped most were the friends who understood that. They'd come over and watch a movie with me, or go thrift-store shopping, some mindless activity that gave me company but didn't require real interaction. It also helped to have other people take over some of the practical details of my life. I was very spacey and unable to focus for a while. And phone calls that had emotional significance to me – having to call the credit card company, etc and say that my husband had died, for instance – were easier for others. I always offer to make those kinds of calls for my friends who are grieving now. They're easy for me, and I know they can feel overwhelming during grief. In a way grieving reminds me a lot of being pregnant – the thing you're really doing is happening deep inside you, and taking your energy and attention, even if you're not consciously thinking about it. You are grieving more than you're doing anything else – that is what you're accomplishing, even while you go through the motions of the rest of your life.

I remember that six months after my husband died felt especially hard. Others who missed him seemed to be moving on, and seemed to expect me to be done grieving. Or maybe I put that pressure on myself. But I felt I was just beginning to grieve then, in a way. My spaciness had gone, and I sort of woke up and realized, truly, that my husband wasn't coming back, and that life as I knew it wouldn't be returning. I was twenty-nine when my husband died, so most of my friends hadn't experienced that kind of loss yet. My parents hadn't either. But acquaintances and strangers emerged. I remember talking to a woman who owned a bookstore I wandered into about her husband's death, and talking to my auto insurance agent about the death of his son. These intimate conversations with strangers were warm lights for me. Those who were further along in grief gave me hope that I could find a life for myself again too, that I wouldn't always feel empty.

Another thing that helped me immensely was my job as a sixth-grade teacher. There are probably many jobs that would feel meaningless after a death, but teaching kids isn't one of them. I remember feeling like work was my eight-hour vacation from my life. I'd walk in the door, and the kids would rush toward me, and I would become completely absorbed in the day, in teaching them and helping them and being amused by them. I'd say any activity that forces you to be in the moment for an extended period of time is great. It's also nice to spend time doing the things that were yours separate from your spouse. I didn't miss my husband while I was teaching, because he'd never been a part of that experience. Exercise was good. Taking trips with friends was good, though walking in the front door when I came home always hit hard.

I also remember that about two years after my husband died was another rough time. I felt guilty that I was enjoying life again, and worried I'd forget him. That passed, but I can't remember when I shifted to feeling like I wouldn't forget him, and being secure in the fact that I'd loved him, and yet also very comfortable being fully in the life I have now.

My first husband died almost fifteen years ago now. I am remarried, and I have two children, and I am very rooted in the life I am leading now. I do think my experience with my first husband's illness, and his death, have deeply influenced the way I live. I joke with my second husband that I appreciate him more than he can ever understand, but it's true. I know what it would mean to lose him, and I'm aware that I could lose him – so I enjoy what I've got while I've got it. I'm not worried or morbid about it, but death is in my consciousness in a very different way than it was before I lost my first husband. I think it allows me (or forces me?) to appreciate my life and the people I love vividly, rather than taking them for granted. I also appreciate my health, and am not angry or resentful when something goes wrong with it. Not to say that I'm happy about it, but after my experience with my first husband, good health feels like incredible good luck rather than the bottom line.

I met my second husband only a year after my first husband died, so I was still in the midst of grieving. Luckily, my second husband wasn't threatened by this – he was more self-possessed and less selfish than I probably would have been. Because of this, I was able to not cut my past off while moving on to the present, which has enriched my life a lot. I am still close to my first husband's family. They still come to my parents' for Christmas, and I take my kids and second husband to visit them often. My kids know about my life with my first husband. I appreciate everyone's willingness to be in this new life together. It can be painful and complicated, but it brings richness to all of our lives, I think.

I wish I could offer a perspective that would make grief easier. I don't know that there is one, except it's worth knowing that it does get better with time. Everyone tells you this, of course, but it's so hard to believe. But it's good to understand that you don't have to forget the person you've loved, or move on in that sense, but that eventually, though it can take years, you will be able to think of them and feel love rather than pain.

As a caregiver, it's also easy to feel a loss of a sense of purpose. You've been working so hard to help keep someone alive, or to make their life meaningful, and now no one needs you. There's a terrible emptiness in that, even if there is also some freedom. But I think it's important to remember that from your experience you know what it feels like to have a sense of purpose, which means that you're ahead of many people. If you know what it feels like, you'll yearn for it again, and eventually you will find it in some other way. It doesn't have to relate to caregiving at all, but you will probably look for, and therefore find, something that brings deep meaning to your life.
--Elizabeth Scarboro, author of *My Foreign Cities*

"I'm Okay" Worksheets

On the next few pages, you'll find weekly worksheets you can use during your first two months after caregiving ends. The worksheets remind you that you are okay.

Each worksheet includes a prompt from me which highlights something you already have for each day of the week. In essence, you already have something which makes you okay, regardless of how bad or difficult the day may have been. Use my prompt to start your day. Then, at the end of the day, add your own reason why you are okay. The worksheet also asks you to take time to reflect after each week and then record what you realized.

My "Okays" for Week One:

Day One
Today, you will be okay because there's enough tissue in the world for your tears.

Today, I am okay because

Day Two
Today, you will be okay because you have enough blankets to warm your cold.

Today I am okay because

Day Three
Today, you will be okay because you have enough clean clothes.

Today I am okay because

Day Four
Today, you will be okay because you have made it this far.

Today I am okay because

Day Five
Today, you will be okay because you are needed.

Today I am okay because

Day Six
Today, you will be okay because you are strong enough to complete a task today.

Today, I am okay because

Day Seven
Today, you will be okay because nature, with its changing seasons, reminds us nothing (including our pain) is permanent.

Today, I am okay because

This week, I realized:

My "Okays" for Week Two:

Day Eight
Today, you will be okay because you are loved.

Today, I am okay because

Day Nine
Today, you will be okay because you have what's needed to get through.

Today I am okay because

Day Ten
Today, you will be okay because you can take it one minute at a time.

Today I am okay because

Day Eleven
Today, you will be okay because you don't need to figure it all out today.

Today I am okay because

Day Twelve
Today, you will be okay because you can call a friend.

Today I am okay because

Day Thirteen
Today, you will be okay because you can take a walk.

Today, I am okay because

Day Fourteen
Today, you will be okay because someone else will understand your pain.

Today, I am okay because

This week, I understood:

My "Okays" for Week Three:

Day Fifteen
Today, you will be okay because you are trusted.

Today, I am okay because

Day Sixteen
Today, you will be okay because you can do for another.

Today I am okay because

Day Seventeen
Today, you will be okay because there's enough sad movies you can watch.

Today I am okay because

Day Eighteen
Today, you will be okay because healing will come.

Today I am okay because

Day Nineteen
Today, you will be okay because your grief will be patient with you.

Today I am okay because

Day Twenty
Today, you will be okay because you can buy flowers.

Today, I am okay because

Day Twenty-One
Today, you will be okay because the world will wait for you.

Today, I am okay because

This week, I found:

My "Okays" for Week Four:

Day Twenty-Two
Today, you will be okay because your pain will teach.

Today, I am okay because

Day Twenty-Three
Today, you will be okay because you can enjoy a delicious treat.

Today I am okay because

Day Twenty-Four
Today, you will be okay because you can close your eyes at any time and see better.

Today I am okay because

Day Twenty-Five
Today, you will be okay because you can redefine hope.

Today, I am okay because

Day Twenty-Six
Today, you will be okay because you can read a great book.

Today, I am okay because

Day Twenty-Seven
Today, you will be okay because you can curl up on the couch at the end of your day.

Today, I am okay because

Day Twenty-Eight
Today, you will be okay because you can check off one item from your To Do list.

Today, I am okay because

This week, I understood:

My "Okays" for Week Five:

Day Twenty-Nine
Today, you will be okay because the sun shines after a storm.

Today, I am okay because

Day Thirty
Today, you will be okay because you can take comfort in your memories.

Today I am okay because

Day Thirty-One
Today, you will be okay because you can change whatever you want.

Today I am okay because

Day Thirty-Two
Today, you will be okay because you have choices.

Today I am okay because

Day Thirty-Three
Today, you will be okay because your heart will heal.

Today I am okay because

Day Thirty-Four
Today, you will be okay because spring arrives after winter.

Today, I am okay because

Day Thirty-Five
Today, you will be okay because you have the energy to get through today.

Today, I am okay because

This week, I know:

My "Okays" for Week Six:

Day Thirty-Six
Today, you will be okay because you have resilience.

Today, I am okay because

Day Thirty-Seven
Today, you will be okay because you can comfort yourself.

Today I am okay because

Day Thirty-Eight
Today, you will be okay because you can reach out for help.

Today I am okay because

Day Thirty-Nine
Today, you will be okay because you can receive blessings.

Today I am okay because

Day Forty
Today, you will be okay because you will find something beautiful today.

Today I am okay because

Day Forty-One
Today, you will be okay because you are strong.

Today, I am okay because

Day Forty-Two
Today, you will be okay because laughter always lives.

Today, I am okay because

This week, I understood:

My "Okays" for Week Seven:

Day Forty-Three
Today, you will be okay because you can count on the sun rising and the sun setting.

Today, I am okay because

Day Forty-Four
Today, you will be okay because you have a piece of knowledge that will come in handy.

Today I am okay because

Day Forty-Five
Today, you will be okay because you have time.

Today I am okay because

Day Forty-Six
Today, you will be okay because you can tell your story to your journal.

Today I am okay because

Day Forty-Seven
Today, you will be okay because you can plan for a tomorrow.

Today I am okay because

Day Forty-Eight
Today, you will be okay because you can light a candle.

Today, I am okay because

Day Forty-Nine
Today, you will be okay because you can find inspiration in the accomplishments of others.

Today, I am okay because

This week, I did these things well:

My "Okays" for Week Eight:

Day Fifty
Today, you will be okay because a life is worth celebrating.

Today, I am okay because

Day Fifty-One
Today, you will be okay because you have a chance.

Today I am okay because

Day Fifty-Two
Today, you will be okay because you can wave "hello" to a neighbor.

Today I am okay because

Day Fifty-Three
Today, you will be okay because you can learn.

Today I am okay because

Day Fifty-Four
Today, you will be okay because you can cook a special meal.

Today I am okay because

Day Fifty-Five
Today, you will be okay because you can say a prayer.

Today, I am okay because

Day Fifty-Six
Today, you will be okay because you can take a few hours off.

Today, I am okay because

This week, I understood:

Your Care Plan

To help you face each day, I've created a care plan that's just for you. The care plan focuses on your WELL—what keeps you well. Your wellness is a combination of wisdom, energy, love and laughter. (You may recognize this care plan; I created a similar one for family caregivers which is available on CareGiving.com. This one is just for you after caregiving ends.) Complete a weekly care plan on Friday or Saturday so that you're ready when Sunday arrives. Your care plan puts your attention on what you want and gets your commitment to get what you need.

My Care Plan
for the Week of (Insert the Week)

My care plan focuses on my WELL:

    1. Wisdom comes from being attentive, grateful and curious.
    2. Energy comes from my food, my exercise and my physical, mental, spiritual and emotional breaks.
    3. Laughter comes from within myself, from my relationships and from my entertainment.
    4. Love comes from within myself, from my relationships and from my passions.

And, to keep me from falling into the well, I'll also take comfort in knowing that this time of my life is a process and a transition which needs my time. I am free to experiment, to fail, to succeed, and to change what no longer works into what works.

During the week of (insert the week), I make the following commitments to staying WELL:

I stay attentive to:

I am grateful for:

I am curious about:

My food choices include:

My exercise routine is:

My Care Plan, Page 2

I will experiment:

- with these social activities:
- with these ideas about my purposes:
- with these ideas about about my gifts:
- with these ideas about my passions:

I laugh about:

I laugh with:

I laugh while:

I love when I:

I love:

I love participating in these activities:

I forgive:

I am working on forgiving:

Signed: Date:

My Care Plan
for the Week of January 1

My care plan focuses on my WELL:

    1. Wisdom comes from being attentive, grateful and curious.
    2. Energy comes from my food, my exercise and my physical, mental, spiritual and emotional breaks.
    3. Laughter comes from within myself, from my relationships and from my entertainment.

4. Love comes from within myself, from my relationships and from my passions.

And, to keep me from falling into the well, I'll also take comfort in knowing that this time of my life is a process and a transition which needs my time. I am free to experiment, to fail, to succeed, and to change what no longer works into what works.

During the week of January 1, I make the following commitments to staying WELL:

I stay attentive to: *When I need to take a break from being with others. I realize I need time to myself.*

I am grateful for: *My caree, who taught me so much. Today, which gives me so many possibilities.*

I am curious about: *What if I got up 30 minutes earlier? Would my day feel less rushed? How did that member of my support group find a job so quickly? (I will ask her for suggestions.)*

My food choices include: *Fruit for snacks, three vegetables a day, one dessert a week.*

My exercise routine is: *I walk 3 miles 6 days a week.*

My Care Plan, Page 2

I will experiment:

- with these social activities: *I'll stay after church for coffee and socializing*
- with these ideas about my purposes: *I'll test out volunteering at our senior center*
- with these ideas about about my gifts: *I'll spend time every Saturday afternoon with my photography*
- with these ideas about my passions: *I'll spend time on Sunday afternoons with my grandkids*

I laugh about: *the good times I shared with my caree, whatever strikes me as being funny*

I laugh with: *my family and friends and during Modern Family on Wednesday evenings and reruns of Friends*

I laugh while: *I am sharing a story about something embarrassing that happened*

I love when I: *take a walk, get a manicure/pedicure*

I love: *being with my family and enjoying a quiet Sunday morning with coffee and the newspaper. I also love to watch CBS Sunday Morning and 60 Minutes*

I love participating in these activities: *lunch with friends, church, monthly book club*

I forgive: *my friends for disappointing me*

I am working on forgiving: *myself when I struggle to forgive others. I sometimes hold onto a grudge too long*

Signed: Date:

The Godspeed Caregiver
(Stage Six in The Caregiving Years, Six Stages to a Meaningful Journey)

Stage 6: The Godspeed Caregiver
My caregiving has ended.

Who are you?
Your role as caregiver ended more than two years ago. You find yourself compelled to make a difference in the lives of other family caregivers. You share information readily with family caregivers in the earlier stages or you start a business dedicated to helping family caregivers or you find a job in which you assist family caregivers. And, you treasure each relationship you have in your life, recognizing that each day, and your health, should never be taken for granted.

Your Keyword: Treasure
--Treasure your dreams;
--Treasure your challenges which led to your opportunities and new skills;
--Treasure your opportunities to share lessons learned;
--Treasure memories of your caree.

Your Challenge
To integrate your former role as a family caregiver into your new life

Your Purpose
To implement your lessons learned from your role as family caregiver, from your caree and from your family members and friends. During this stage, which can last as long you wish, even your lifetime, you reap the benefits of your efforts.

As a "Godspeed Caregiver," what can you do?
1. Follow your dreams.
Make your goals a reality.

2. Family caregivers will look to you as a mentor and leader.
Allow family caregivers in earlier stages the same freedom to stumble and steady themselves that you had. Share your experiences with the family caregivers behind you. They can learn from you.

3. Treasure the memories you have of your caree.
Continue to remember your caree regularly through rituals, such as enjoying an ice cream cone in her honor on her birthday, or by planting trees in his honor. Reading and reviewing your diary will be a great way to remember.
   Of course, your best memorial to your caree's memory is a life you build for yourself filled with healthy relationships, productive careers and joy and laughter.

4. An apple a day…
Your apples (your healthy activities, relationships, perspectives) kept you going during your caregiving experience. Now, consider how you'll use them to create your future. How did your apples change? How did you change? What would you like to try next?

Go for it. The world is your apple.

Resources

After Death Checklists

Death and Finances: Eight Things To Do After a Loved One Passes: www.dailyfinance.com/2011/02/14/death-and-finances-eight-things-to-do-after-a-loved-one-passes/

What To Do When a Loved One Dies: www.aarp.org/home-family/friends-family/info-06-2012/when-loved-one-dies-checklist.html

What to Do When a Loved One Dies: www.consumerreports.org/cro/magazine/2012/10/what-to-do-when-a-loved-one-dies/index.htm

Business Resources

Chris Brogan's blog: www.chrisbrogan.com

Entrepreneur: www.entrepreneur.com

Harvard Business Review: www.hbr.org

Help a Reporter Out: www.helpareporter.com

Service Corps of Retire Executives (SCORE): www.score.org

Seth Godin's blog: www.sethgodin.com/sg

The U. S. Small Business Administration: www.sba.gov

Career Resources

AARP: www.aarp.org/work/

CareerBuilder: www.careerbuilder.com/JobSeeker/Resources/CareerResources.aspx

The 40-Year-Old Intern: www.hbr.org/2012/11/the-40-year-old-intern/

Monster: career-advice.monster.com

Returning to Work: www.irelaunch.com

Returning to Work After Caring for an Aging Parent: articles.washingtonpost.com/2009-02-20/jobs/36867357_1_care-parents-simple-answer

A Sandwiched Caregiver Returns Back to Work: parenting.blogs.nytimes.com/2012/05/07/a-sandwich-generation-caregiver-heads-back-to-work

Seven Keys to Rejoining the Workforce After a Long Break: www.forbes.com/sites/susanadams/2012/11/20/7-keys-to-rejoining-the-workforce-after-a-long-break/

Closing out the House

Who Gets Grandma's Yellow Pie Plate?™ www1.extension.umn.edu/family/personal-finance/who-gets-grandmas-yellow-pie-plate/

Podcast: The Stuff of Battles: www.blogtalkradio.com/caregiving/2010/09/22/the-stuff-of-battles

Podcast: Stuff That Stuffs: www.blogtalkradio.com/caregiving/2010/09/09/stuff-that-stuffs

National Association of Senior Move Managers: www.nasmm.org

Credit Reporting Agencies

Equifax (www.equifax.com)
P.O. Box 740241
Atlanta, GA 30374-0241
1-800-685-1111

Experian (www.experian.com)
P.O. Box 2104
Allen, TX 75013-0949
1-888-EXPERIAN (397-3742)

Trans Union (www.transunion.com)
P.O. Box 1000
Chester, PA 19022
1-800-916-8800

Debt

Approved counseling services by the U. S. Justice Department: www.justice.gov/ust/eo/bapcpa/ccde/cc_approved.htm

Who Pays Off Credit Card Debt After a Death: money.msn.com/credit-cards/who-pays-off-credit-card-debt-after-a-death

Finding a Job

Care.com: www.care.com

Elance.com: www.elance.com

Guru.com: www.guru.com

Lyft: www.lyft.com

Sitter City: www.sittercity.com

Snag a Job: www.snagajob.com

Social Media How-To's: www.mashable.com/how-to

Task Rabbit: www.taskrabbit.com

Low Cost Health Care

Health Resources and Services Administration of U.S. Department of Health and Human Services: findahealthcenter.hrsa.gov/Search_HCC.aspx

Grieving

The Center for Complicated Grief: www.complicatedgrief.org

Compassionate Friends (grieving support after the loss of a child): www.compassionatefriends.org/home.aspx

Coping with Grief and Loss: www.helpguide.org/mental/grief_loss.htm

GriefShare (community support groups and seminars): www.griefshare.org

In the Presence of All Souls: www.nytimes.com/2013/10/31/opinion/in-the-presence-of-all-souls.html

Mental Health America: www.nmha.org/go/information/get-info/grief-and-bereavement

National Bereavement Resource Guide: www.moyerfoundation.org/nbrg/default.aspx

Podcast: After Death, Where Does the Hope Go? www.blogtalkradio.com/caregiving/2013/07/16/after-death-where-does-the-hope-go

Podcast: Book Club Discussion: "Miraculous Moments: True Stories Affirming That Life Goes On" by Elissa Al-Chokhachy: www.blogtalkradio.com/caregiving/2011/04/26/book-club

Podcast: Grieving: www.blogtalkradio.com/caregiving/2011/01/25/grieving

"Replacement Therapy" by Donna Webb: www.caregiving.com/2010/08/replacement-therapy/

Learning

Classes: www.coursera.org

Crafts: www.craftsy.com

Crafts: www.craftdaily.com

Culture and Learning: www.openculture.com

Hobbies: www.dabble.co

Meetup: www.meetup.com

Online degrees: www.phoenix.edu

Podcasts: Interviews with Former Family Caregivers

After Caregiving Ends, How Do You Reconcile Caregiving? www.blogtalkradio.com/aftergiving/2013/06/12/after-caregiving-ends-how-do-you-reconcile-what-happened

After Caregiving: The Perspective of a Year: www.blogtalkradio.com/caregiving/2010/09/25/table-talk-1

After Caregiving: The First Year: www.blogtalkradio.com/aftergiving/2013/05/15/the-first-year

A Business Life After a Caregiving Life: www.blogtalkradio.com/caregiving/2010/09/16/life-after-caregiving

Book Club, "Julita's Sands, A Memoir," by Emily Placido: www.blogtalkradio.com/caregiving/2010/10/26/book-club

Life After Caregiving: Donna: www.blogtalkradio.com/caregiving/2010/10/30/table-talk-donna-w

Life After Caregiving: Kristin: www.blogtalkradio.com/caregiving/2012/10/29/life-after-caregiving-kristin

Life After Caregiving: Laura (aka "Roaringmouse"): www.blogtalkradio.com/caregiving/2013/06/20/life-after-caregiving-an-update-from-roaringmouse

Managing the First Year After Caregiving Ends: www.blogtalkradio.com/aftergiving/2013/10/18/managing-the-first-year-after-caregiving-ends

Post-Traumatic Stress Disorder Resources

National Alliance on Mental Illness: www.nami.org/Template.cfm?Section=posttraumatic_stress_disorder

National Institute of Mental Health: www.nimh.nih.gov/health/topics/post-traumatic-stress-disorder-ptsd/index.shtml

National Center for PTSD: www.ptsd.va.gov

Self Publishing

Blurb: www.blurb.com

Create Space: www.createspace.com

Lulu: www.lulu.com

Outskirts Press: www.outskirtspress.com

Smashwords: www.smashwords.com

Setting the Estate

American Bar Association's Guide to Wills and Estates: www.americanbar.org/groups/public_education/publications/books_related_products/the_aba_guide_towillsestates.html

Deactivating, Deleting and Memorializing Facebook Accounts: www.facebook.com/help/359046244166395

Podcast: After Caregiving, Settling Your Caree's Estate: www.blogtalkradio.com/caregiving/2013/06/06/settling-your-carees-estate

Travel

Independent Traveler: www.independenttraveler.com

Frommer's Travel Guides: www.frommers.com

Rick Steves: www.ricksteves.com

Road Scholar: www.roadscholar.org

Values

Personal Growth: How to Align Your Values and Your Life: www.psychologytoday.com/blog/the-power-prime/201205/personal-growth-how-align-your-values-and-your-life

The Power of Personal Values by Roy Posner: www.gurusoftware.com/GuruNet/Personal/Topics/Values.htm

Books

Cleaning Out a House

How to Clean Out Your Parent's Estate in 30 Days or Less by Julie Hall

Sell, Keep or Toss? How to Downsize a Home, Settle an Estate, and Appraise Personal Property by Harry L Rinker

Debt

How to Get Out of Debt, Stay Out of Debt, and Live Prosperously: Based on the Proven Principles and Techniques of Debtors Anonymous* by Jerrold Mundis

Difficult Transitions

Tough Times: Navigating Your Way Through Difficult Times by Elizabeth Harper Neeld

What's Next? Navigating Transitions to Make the Rest of Your Life Count by H. Norman Wright

Grieving

Blue Nights by Joan Didion

Chicken Soup for the Soul: Grieving and Recovery: 101 Inspirational and Comforting Stories about Surviving the Loss of a Loved One by Jack Canfield, Mark Victor Hansen, Amy Newmark

Don't Take My Grief Away From Me by Doug Manning

On Grief and Grieving: Finding the Meaning of Grief Through the Five Stages of Loss by Elisabeth Kubler-Ross, David A. Kessler

The Grief Recovery Handbook, 20th Anniversary Expanded Edition: The Action Program for Moving Beyond Death, Divorce, and Other Losses including Health, Career, and Faith by John W. James

Healing After Loss (Daily Meditations) by Martha W. Hickman

How to Go On Living When Someone You Love Dies by Therese A Rando

Laughter, Tears and Braids: A father's Journey Through Losing His Wife to Cancer by Bruce Ham
Life After Loss: A Practical Guide to Renewing Your Life after Experiencing Major Loss by Bob Deits

Life After Loss: Conquering Grief and Finding Hope by Raymond Moody, Dianne Arcangel

Loving from the Outside In, Mourning from the Inside Out by Alan D. Wolfelt

A New Normal: Learning to Live with Grief and Loss by Darlene Cross MS MFT

The Orphaned Adult: Understanding And Coping With Grief And Change After The Death Of Our Parents by Alexander Levy

Praying Our Goodbyes by Joyce Rupp

The Way Of Transition: Embracing Life's Most Difficult Moments by William Bridges

When Parents Die by Edward Myers

The Year of Magical Thinking by Joan Didion

Life After Death

Proof of Heaven: A Neurosurgeon's Journey into the Afterlife by Eben Alexander

When Will the Heaven Begin? This Is Ben Breedlove's Story by Ally Breedlove and Ken Abraham

Personal Growth

Choose Yourself by James Altucher

The 15 Invaluable Laws of Growth: Live Them and Reach Your Potential by John C. Maxwell

Start with Why: How Great Leaders Inspire Everyone to Take Action by Simon Sinek

Your Life Calling: Reimagining the Rest of Your Life by Jane Pauley

Settling an Estate

American Bar Association Guide to Wills and Estates, Fourth Edition: Everything You Need to Know about Wills, Estates, Trusts, and Taxes
The Settlement Game: How to Settle an Estate Peacefully and Fairly by Angie Epting Morris

Transitions

Transitions: Prayers and Declarations for a Changing Life by Julia Cameron

About the Author

Denise M. Brown, Professional Caregiving Coach and Speaker, began working with family caregivers in 1990. She was an early developer of online support groups for family caregivers and former family caregivers, launching her first in 1996 through her website, CareGiving.com.

Denise sold CareGiving.com in March 2020 to focus her work on developing and leading training programs. Denise developed the Certified Caregiving Advocate, Consultant, Educator, Facilitator and Specialist programs to empower and train family caregivers and former family caregivers. She also created the Certified Family Care Manager program to arm family caregivers with the skills and techniques they need to care for their family members.

To reach Denise, please visit careyearsacademy.com.

Made in the USA
Coppell, TX
11 November 2021